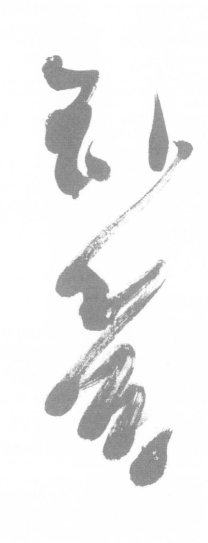

THE WAY TO BECOME A PERSON IN HEAVEN WHILE LIVING
by Woo Myung

First published in Korean September 2006
Fifth printing Aug 2007
English edition May 2009

Published by CHAM Publishing Company, President Chang Hee Choi
Hapjeongdong 360-1, Mapoku, Seoul 121-884, Korea
Phone        82-2-325-4192~4
Facsimile    82-2-325-1569
E-mail       chambooks@maum.org
Korean Registration No.13-1147, Date 2000. 12. 29

ISBN        978-89-87523-22-4(03100)

        This book has been translated into English
        from the original 'The Way to Become a Person in Heaven While Living'
        written in Korean in 2006.
        Translated and edited by
        Sun Hae Cho, Caroline Choi, Margie Conboy, Joe Gattis, Myung Hyun Hong,
        Mi Young Jung, Susan J. Lee
        For more information about Maum Meditation, go to http://www.maum.org

# The Way To Become A Person In Heaven While Living

Woo Myung

CHAM PUBLISHING CO.

# contents

chapter one   The Real And The False

The Way To Become A Person In Heaven While Living ^018 |

The Real And The Fake ^021 | What Is Human Sin And Karma? ^024 | The Difference

Between The Living And The Dead Is The Same As The Difference Between Heaven

And Earth ^029 | Come To Truth ^031 | The Kingdom Of The Soul And Spirit Where All

Creations Live ^032 | From The World Of Hardships To A World Free Of It ^035 | Live As

The True Shape ^038 | Among The Ordinary There Is The Extraordinary ^040 |

Completion Is To Accomplish All And To Be Fully Enlightened ^043 | Death ^048 |

Only A Person Who Has Become Truth Lives ^049 | The Kingdom Of Light ^055 |

The Difference Between One Who Cleanses And One Who Has Accomplished ^056 |

The Master Is The Universe. All Creations Are Also The Master ^057 | Truth And

Man Are Not Separate ^061 | An Enlightened Person Is Silent ^063 | Enlightenment Is

Believing, Living, Knowing All Scriptures, And Going To Eternal Heaven ^064 | When

One's Consciousness Becomes That Of Truth ^067 | The Living And The Dead ^069 |

What Is True? What Is False? ^071 | What Is Maum Meditation? ^072 |

What Is Wisdom? ^075 | We Must Be Reborn As The Holy Ghost ^076 |

What People Know [077] | To Set Free [079] | Do Not Be Loyal To Your Body Which Will Rot Away [080] | You Can Only Go To Heaven And Live Forever Without Life And Death While You Are Living.You Cannot Go There After Death [082] | One Who Is Completely Enlightened.One Who Has Accomplished All.One Who Knows All [085] | The Living World [086] | The Master [089] | People Mistake Themselves As Buddha [091] | The Absurd Seeking Heaven In Shapes And In The Material World [092] | The River Is Silent [095] | One Who Is Accomplished [098] | Who Will Accuse Whom? Who Will Blame Whom? [099] | Enlightenment [100] | Light [101] | One Receives Divine Blessings Only Through Absolution Of One's Sins [104] | Resurrection [107] | Truth Is Universally Valid, Not Magic [108] | The Way To Heaven [111] | Enlightenment Comes Only When You Become Truth [114] | You Will Not Know What You Have Not Realized Because Your Mind Is Unable To Accept [117] | There Is Nothing Above Truth.There Is Nothing Greater Than Truth.That Which Is Not In The Kingdom Of Truth Is Hell, False, Delusional [120] | One Can Teach Only What He Has And That Is All That Can Be Learned From Him [124] | Truth, God, Divinity, Buddha, The Creator, Allah.All Are

The True Existence [126] | What Is The New World? What Is The New Heaven And New Earth? Where Are They? [129] | The Difference Between What Is True And What Is False [131] | Wanderer [132] | Enlightenment Is Faith [133] | Only People Who Go To Heaven While Living Can Live In Heaven [137] | Only Those Who Go To Heaven While Living Can Go To Heaven [142] | Real And Fake [144] | Everything Is Made By The Mind [146] | People Living In A Dream Do Not Know They Are In A Dream [148] | Truth Is As It Is [150] |

# chapter two    Why Humans Live And What Humans Live For

People Can Neither See Nor Hear What They Do Not Have 156 | Eternal Life And Heaven Must Be A Reality. One Who Is Not Complete Now, One Who Does Not Have Heaven And Eternal Life Now, Cannot Go To Heaven After He Dies Because He Does Not Have Heaven 157 | Only When The True Existence Comes As A Human Can Mankind Become Truth 160 | People's Conceptions And Behaviors 163 | The Most Important Thing In The World 166 | The Reason And Purpose Of Life 169 | One Lives According To What He Has Within The Mind 173 | Truth Can Only Be Known By One Who Has Truth Within 177 | One World 178 | Heaven And Hell 179 | The Definition Of The Sky 180 | Only The Savior Can Provide Salvation 182 | True And False 187 | What Is Sin? 190 | Nature 192 | True Love 194 | Great Mercy And Great Compassion 197 | What Is True Compassion? 198 | Nature's Flow 199 | The Ordinary Is Extraordinary. The Ordinary Is The Greatest 201 | Faith Is Enlightenment Of The Mind 203 | Human Completion Is To Be Absolved Of One's Sins 205 | The Method To See, Know, And Become The Existence Of Truth 207 | What Are Blessings? 209 | Truth And The Devil – Good And Evil – Coexist In People's Minds 213 | Now Is The Time For Humans To Be Created And Live 215 | The Existence Of Truth 219 | Great Nature 221 |

What Is Pride? 223 | Story Of Life 225 | An Enlightened Saint Is A Completed Person Who Has Been Reborn As The Existence Of Truth 230 | The Most Important Thing In The World Is To Come Out Of One's Tomb And Live In The Land Of Light 231 | Tales Of Going To Heaven 235 | The Most Urgent Thing In The World 239 | Let Us Live As The Wind 243 | One Must Know Truth After Becoming Truth.Do Not Try To Know Truth Through Your Own Conceptions 247 | Light And Darkness I 249 | The Reason And Purpose Of Human Life 252 | The Will Of The Creator 255 | Vanity Of Life 258 | Trueness And Falseness 260 | God Is Everything 261 | Become Nature And Stay 264 | The True Meaning Of Being Extraordinary 265 | The Most Important Thing In The World 266 | Education Begins With The Recovery Of Mankind's Original Nature 270 | The Wise One 274 | Human Life I 275 | One Who Is Born On The Earth Lives On The Earth.One Who Is Born In Heaven Lives In Heaven 277 | What Is Rebirth And Resurrection? What Is Heaven? 279 | The Soul And Spirit Is The Living Creator, Truth 282 | What Frightens The Devil The Most 284 | The True World 287 | In The Land Of Reality 292 | Memories 294 | The Land That Lives In My Mind 296 |

# chapter three  Human Completion

Stories And Real Life $^{300}$ | A Fine Mind $^{303}$ | It Exists Because It Exists In The

Mind $^{304}$ | Darkness And Brightness $^{305}$ | Humans Are Ghosts $^{306}$ | How To Educate

People So That They May Become Complete $^{308}$ | Our Bodies Should Be Reborn As

The Perfect Mind Of Truth $^{313}$ | The Biggest, Widest, Lowest, And Highest Existence

In The World $^{316}$ | The Will Of God $^{320}$ | The Creator Is A Living Existence, The

Existence Which Lives As It Is $^{322}$ | What Is The Mind? $^{326}$ | When You Become

Truth $^{330}$ | Blessings $^{331}$ | Trueness In The Mind $^{334}$ | Revelation $^{335}$ | Maum

Meditation Is About Becoming Truth, The True Mind.The Proof That One Has

Become Truth Is... $^{339}$ | The Life Of A Person Who Is Alive $^{344}$ | Eternal Life $^{345}$ |

Conversations With God $^{349}$ | Resurrection $^{353}$ | The True Meaning Of The Phrase,

'Jal Moshida' $^{355}$ | The Reason We Must Discard Our Minds Is Because Everything

That Has Happened In The World And Everything That Exists In The World Are

Delusions $^{357}$ | God's Mind $^{358}$ | Light And Darkness II $^{361}$ | Are You Complete? $^{363}$ |

Only One Whose Mind Is Reborn As Truth Will Live.He Will Live Because He Is

Truth $^{364}$ | Let Only Truth Remain In The Mind $^{365}$ | Recovery Of Man's Original

Nature $^{366}$ | Only One Who Is Reborn As The Energy And Light Of The Universe

Will Live 367 | Why Don't You Try Cleansing Your Mind? 368 | A Rich Mind 369 |

The Years 370 | People Live According To What They Have In The Mind 372 |

Our Bodies And Minds Must Be Reborn As Truth Of The Universe 373 | Human

Completion 376 | Drinking 377 | Our Capacity For Receiving Blessings 382 |

True Riches 384 | What Does It Mean To Be Righteous? 387 | One Who Is Reborn

As The Holy Ghost 390 | Infinity Is… 392 | Ghosts 394 | How To Speak To People

According To Their Situation 398 | Even Though The Words Are Different, Buddha

And God Are The Existence Of Truth And Are One 400 | Humans Can Become Truth

When There Is A Human Who Is Truth 401 | Life 402 | Duckweed 403 | The Difference

Between A Ghost And True God 406 | Human Life II 409 |

# The Way To
# Become A Person
# In Heaven
## While Living

Woo Myung

# Preface

For so long, people have not been able to distinguish between what is true and what is false. Trueness, or Truth, is an entity that is everlasting and never-changing, an entity that is alive, the universe itself, or in other words, the world. Falseness is the world of the human mind, which humans possess in their minds by taking pictures of the world with their minds. Due to the fact that people live in their own false worlds, human completion can be achieved only when they come out from their own minds, which are false, and are reborn in the real world. This is when humans become complete.

Religion, philosophy and academics will all be made right and people will be able to live well and live happily. People have learned only false things in a false world, and thus do not know what is true. Consequently, they live with suffering and burdens.

Only one who is true knows both what is true and what is false; but one who is false lives knowing neither. Therefore, his consciousness is dead. Ask yourselves, if I cannot become or have yet to become true at the place I go to in order to become true, then isn't that place false? It is most likely that only a place, where one is in the process of becoming or have already become true, is true.

The completion of humans is achieved when both the false world as well as one's self (me) that lives in that world no longer exist, and one is reborn in the real world. The time for the completion of humans is at hand, but man's consciousness is bound to his preconceptions and habits and lives without knowing what is true. Therefore man is dead and lives without knowing he is dead.

A method to come out of one's false world and become real exists here, in this world. Therefore I write this book in the hopes that everyone will become true and become reborn in the complete new world. When many people become true, when their lives become one, and when they live as Truth, there will be eternal life.

Woo Myung

About the Author

Woo Myung, best-selling South Korean author of many books about Truth, achieved enlightenment after deep introspection about life and existence. When he became Truth, he dedicated his life to teaching others to become Truth and founded Maum Meditation. For his efforts, he was awarded the Mahatma Gandhi Peace Award by the United Nations International Association of Educators for World Peace (IAEWP) in September of 2002. Woo Myung has also been appointed as a United Nations World Peace Ambassador.

He is the author of numerous books including Wisdom For Life(1996), The Natural Flow Of The Universe(1998), True Mind(1998), The Enlightened World(1998), World Beyond World(2003), The Forever Living World(2004), The Formula From Heaven That Will Save The World(2005), The Way To Become A Person In Heaven While Living(2006), World Beyond World(English edition, 2005) and The Place Where One Becomes Real Is The Real Place(2008) .

Translator's Note

Generally, the Korean word 'maum' is quite often translated as being the word 'mind,' as does throughout the entirety of this book. However, in all actuality the word 'maum' refers to a much broader mental, spiritual entity, in which case the word maum not only means 'mind' but also 'heart' – as in 'one must be true at heart' or 'we know in our hearts.' Therefore, the reader would benefit to know that the word 'mind' read throughout this book means both 'mind' and 'heart.'

When you look upon the universe with clear and true mind

The universe is living; the universe is in you

Woo Myung

# chapter one

## The Real And The False

# The Way To Become A Person In Heaven While Living

## The Way To Heaven While Living

People commonly believe that they will go to heaven after they die and that bad people will go to hell after they die. People living in this world do not know that this world is hell; therefore, they also do not know about heaven. This is because people who live in heaven know both heaven and hell, but people who live in hell know neither.

When people live in the world, they live by sustaining their bodies with the energy from food. However, in order to live forever even after the body passes away, one must be reborn as Truth, the energy and God of the universe. This existence is the universe before the universe, which does not have a beginning or end; this existence does not have death; this existence is living, and it is the soul and spirit, itself. One who is reborn as this existence has no death because he is reborn as Truth. When he becomes the forever-living, never-dying God, he lives in the kingdom of Truth, heaven. Humans cannot live forever without becoming this existence while living.

The method for humans to go to eternal heaven while

living is to cleanse the self-centered body and mind from this
great universe and even cleanse their false conceptions of the
universe. Then the pure universe remains. This existence is
Truth. When you are reborn as the body and mind of this
existence, that kingdom is the everlasting land and heaven.
This existence existed before the beginning and exists after the
beginning; it is self-existing and exists as it is. The emptiness
of this existence is where God exists. People cannot get rid of
it no matter how hard they try. People cannot see this living
existence because people see only what they have in their
minds. They cannot see or hear the everlasting, never-dying
Truth because they cannot see or hear what they do not have in
their minds. They do not know this existence because they do
not have it. Therefore, they also cannot become this existence.
Only when people become Truth will this world be heaven.
Only then can people live forever.

The method to go to heaven is by cleansing the
body and mind, which is your exact shape and size, as well as
cleansing all the shapes of all creations in this universe. The
Great Soul and Spirit is the place of origin of all creations. This
Great Soul and Spirit is energy and God itself, which are one.

When this Great Soul and Spirit becomes you and is within you, you and Truth are one.

In that kingdom, an individual and the whole are one and the individual will live because it is Truth, which is the whole. In that kingdom, existence and non-existence are one. Even though the body passes away, a person who is reborn in that kingdom can live with his mind, which is the body and mind of Truth. The mind is the shape itself. True mind is Truth. One who has this Truth can live because he is Truth.

The kingdom of Truth is a place where only Truth can live and only what is Truth exists. This is the kingdom where humans cannot live unless they become Truth while living. This is the kingdom where humans cannot live unless they become the soul and spirit of the everlasting, never-changing energy and God.

# The Real And The Fake

I hear a man coughing in the early morning darkness. He goes over the hill to the fields carrying manure on his back. This is the life of a diligent man. When I was young, it was a time of poverty. Everybody had many children without having enough to eat or wear. My mother would say to me, "Hard working people are already out of their beds. It is not good to be lazy."

My youth was a time of wandering. I was not satisfied with the world. I had no money and no family reputation to support me because my family was poor. It was a time when the rich and the obsequious received recognition and advancement. Even government aid was available only to those with connections. I know I am not a clever person and I am dull-witted. But I lived diligently with all my heart, and thus, I became quite wealthy. Although I lived well, I did not like who I was, a person who just ate and lived only for my body. I was always curious about where humans came from, why they live and where they go. I figured that the one lifetime I have here, in this world, is not all there is. The life of a human being is so meaningless and vain and I felt there had to be a different way of living rather than just living this life in such futility. I thought that just living in this world is not all there is to human life. I had questions about why saints are saints and why ordinary people just pass away in vain.

Such questions about the ways of the world and other numerous questions were all solved when my self died and when my mind became the original nature. I was reborn from a narrow human mind to the mind of the Creator. I realized I was Truth, and that I had to let people in the world know Truth and become Truth; I felt bewildered then, for it would be the most difficult task in the world. Thus, for one year I just wrote about Truth, all the while managing my private educational institution. After I started teaching Truth to people, I realized that for humans to become Truth is more difficult than picking a star from the sky.

Before I became Truth, I knew I was the worst person in the world. Therefore I could not laugh heartily and I always scolded myself. While getting people to truly repent, I found that people live without knowing they are sinners, and that they live with a two-faced mind that hides the fact that they are the worst person. People are sinners because they have a self-centered mind. People are sinners because they are not one with Truth. All who do not become Truth are sinners. People who become Truth are those who are reborn as new people through repentance. This is human completion. When people devote themselves to Truth, and when their body and mind are reborn as Truth, all are one as Truth, and thus, there is no death.

People do not know what Truth is and what false is. Truth knows both Truth and falseness. However, the false know neither the false nor Truth. People do not know what Truth is, nor do they know what they are being deceived by. When they have a bigger mind and become Truth, they will know the wisdom of the world and will live without death.

Ask yourself whether or not you are the real one now. If you are not the real one now, you cannot go to the kingdom of Truth and you cannot live because you are not Truth. A person who is false, in other words, a fake person who is not true, will live in the fake world, which is an illusion; and there will be only death because that world is fake and does not exist.

# What Is Human Sin And Karma?

The world consists of the body and mind of the universe, which is the true existence. This true existence is the origin itself, the never-changing, everlasting existence, which creates everything in the universe. This existence is the living, non-material, yet real existence, which existed before infinity, exists now and will exist forever. Because this existence is non-material, people cannot see, hear, touch, smell or taste it. However, this existence is living. Only this existence is forever-living and never-dying. It is the origin, or root, of every creation in the universe. Everything in the universe came forth from this existence. Thus, the shape of this existence is in the form of every creation in the universe.

This existence is the creator and is omnipotent and omniscient; and thus, it created everything in the universe. It is the origin of everything in the universe. Because human beings are self-centered, they are not one with this existence. During the era of incompletion, man could not become one with this existence due to man's self-centered mind. The era of incompletion served its purpose of bringing more humans into this world throughout periods of formation, growth, and fruition.

This false, self-centered mind of humans takes pictures of the world, the perfect kingdom of God, using their eyes, ears, nose, and mouth. These pictures are stored in people's minds and they live in the pictures as the owner of those pictures. In science, we learn that the camera was invented based on the principles of the human eye. Wherever we go, we take pictures of the real existence and then store these pictures in our minds. These pictures are not real; the actual place we visited is real. When we recall a memory, we recall the stored pictures, which are false images of the real thing. Like this, people take pictures of their hometown, friends, parents, relatives, and neighbors, and store all the pictures in their minds.

People take pictures of everything – including elementary school, middle school, high school, college, and everything in society – through seeing with the eyes, hearing with the ears, smelling with the nose, tasting with the mouth, and feeling with the body. Moreover, they store such pictures in their minds. They live through these pictures they have stored in their minds, and thus, they live in the false world, the delusional world, hell. Living within their mind worlds they have created is hell, and all the while people think that they are right based on their fixed beliefs and behaviors.

He who has his own mind world continues to live within his mind world even after death. This mind world is a non-existing delusional world, and thus, it is death. When people become complete, that is, when they become one with Truth, the world is already complete and is the everlasting and never-dying heaven. However, people live trapped in their hell world because they have the hell kingdom that they have made for themselves. For example, the existence of Manhattan is real as it is, but a picture of Manhattan is not the real Manhattan. People live in their mind world as the main character of their movie. There is no life in that film. Discard it. Live as the world. Then you will become a saint, a person with all wisdom who knows nature's logic.

The main character living in that film which is within oneself does not have life, and only lives according to the script. The purpose of Maum Meditation is to teach people how to discard their pictures, which are fake, and enable people to become the world – perfect Truth – and to be reborn in heaven, the living world. It enables one to live as a child of the everlasting, never-dying God, without worries but with freedom. When you discard the false delusional picture world, you will be reborn as Truth, which is the body and mind of the universe and the Great Soul and Great Spirit; and you will go to eternal heaven while living.

The world is already awakened
The world is already complete
But man is trapped within his own mind world
He lives as the owner of his set of pictures
Man is not living in the real world
He is trapped within the hell he has made
This is why he is dead
In order to breathe true life in to those pictures
Burn all the pictures, then only the world remains
When one becomes a person of the world
This means he is born again as Truth
Which is to achieve human completion
Because a person has all his experiences in his mind

He is not one with the world

This is sin and karma

When a person does not have his own mind world

Only the world remains

Because man has not become the world

Because he is not born in the world

He does not live in the world

Being reborn as the body and mind of the world

Being reborn as the everlasting, never-dying God

Is the cleansing of the mind

This is Maum Meditation

# The Difference Between The Living And The Dead Is The Same As The Difference Between Heaven And Earth

The empty universe is the origin of all creations

It is non-existence, but it exists

Therefore, all creations come from this existence

Non-existence brings forth existence

Since people do not have this non-existence within them

They think it does not really exist

But when people have this non-existence in their minds

This non-existence is the soul and spirit

Only this is true life

But they do not know this because they do not have true life

Only this non-existence is living

Only this non-existence is alive

Only one who has become this non-existence lives


One only knows, speaks, and lives

According to what he has within

One who has the universe within him

Knows the true meaning of the universe

Living as the will of the universe by becoming the universe

Is true life

It exists before the wind

It exists before the clouds

It exists before all creations

This itself is Truth and is alive

People do not know it is living

Because they do not have it within their minds

Only this itself is Truth

Only this itself lives

Forever, and ever


The superior, the foolish

The living, the dead

The wise, the unwise

One with Truth, one with false

Such are as different as life and death

As different as heaven and earth

# Come To Truth

If you want to know me

If you want to find me

If you want to see me

If you want to resemble me

If you want to be one with me

Come to heaven

Become heaven

And live with me

In heaven

Eternally without death

Only one whose mind has become heaven

Can see me and know me

Only one whose mind has become heaven is Truth

And can live forever in my kingdom

The forever-living and never-dying God is heaven

With the wisdom of heaven

One can live eternally

With all creations

# The Kingdom Of The Soul And Spirit Where All Creations Live

The eternal, never-dying God is the universe before the universe. This universe is empty but its soul and spirit exists, and therefore, it is the place where the universe is created divinely. All creations in the universe are the embodiment of this soul and spirit. All creations appear in the shape of the universe when the condition is right.

The universe is the Great Soul and Spirit itself. Everything in the universe appears and lives eternally in this kingdom as the Great Soul and Spirit. Because every individual entity itself is the soul and spirit of Truth, it has no death, and the soul and spirit of each individual is living. Thus a person, whose mind becomes Truth while living, can live eternally without death.

Every creation in the universe is already enlightened and all is living in the kingdom of Truth. However, in the minds of human beings, in their souls and spirits, they have stored the attachments, delusions. Therefore human beings are dead because they are not the living soul and spirit of life. There is no soul and spirit of true life within them. A person who is reborn as the soul and spirit of the master of the universe has no death because he has the soul and spirit of the universe. This is eternal life; this is resurrection and this is to live eternally in heaven. Because the individual is reborn as the body and mind of the universe, or Truth, he is the energy and light of the universe; therefore, he has no death.

The reason why we came to this world is to become the eternal never-dying God and to live forever. A mind that has become the never-dying God is a completely empty mind. It is an empty mind without any desires, anguish, anxiety or false thoughts. Although mind does not exist, this mind itself is the mind of the God of wisdom. If a person thinks he knows, then his mind is a delusional one. If he is curious, it is his delusional mind that is curious. If one has curiosity, questions, suspicions, doubts, anguish, anxiety, or false thoughts, or if there is anything he does not know, that is his delusional mind. When there are none of these in one's mind, his mind is the mind of God. That is when the mind knows everything and has no curiosity, questions, suspicions, doubts, anguish, anxiety nor any false thoughts.

The mind of Truth, the Creator, is the Holy Soul and Holy Spirit itself. The individual, who is reborn as the Holy Soul and Holy Spirit, is energy and light itself. He lives with all creations of the universe, in its kingdom, without death. He lives without death because he is reborn with true life, and because the individual is the God of life itself.

It is death itself if one were to die without his soul and spirit being reborn as Truth – the soul and spirit, energy and light of the universe – while living. Only a person who becomes Truth while living can live in the kingdom of Truth. He can live in the living kingdom of Truth without death, because the living soul and spirit of Truth lives in the individual. So do not let go of the one and only chance to live, but rather change your mind into the Great Soul and Spirit of the living Truth of the universe.

The person, who has Truth, the Creator, in his mind, is in heaven because he lives as it is in the living kingdom of Truth. This place is the kingdom of heaven. The person who is the soul and spirit of Truth will live in this kingdom, and the whole universe will live forever.

# From The World Of Hardships To A World Free Of It

Do you find it easy to live in this world?

During a time when the world changes everyday

People cannot keep a steady mind

People are out of their minds

Do you find it easy to live in this world?

When times change

It is difficult to live in such changing times

When times change

One who changes with the times

Has little trouble making ends meet

One who resists the changing times

One who is far from reality

Has trouble making ends meet


Because the world does not follow your selfish expectations

Because the world does not unfold as you please

Your life is difficult

However when you live unbound to

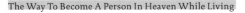

Either living well or living with difficulties

When you live from the world's perspective

And work diligently, just do your work

Live without self

And just live without your self that has difficulty

Then there is no pain, no hell and no anxiety

And you will live a good life

Instead of blaming the world and others

A person must cleanse that mind of his that blames others

Then the world becomes bright, the world becomes one

One who knows that it is not the faults and mistakes of others

But that it is his own fault, and that everything is his own sin

Is the wise one

When you repent your sins

And live as Truth, the true self

The world is heaven, the world will be full of pleasure

It is the one world

Where there is no 'this world', no 'that world'

No matter how hard you try to live for the self

There are no results, there is no meaning or value

But if you live for the world

In the one world

There will be pleasure in the mind

There will be contentment in the mind


Because there is no fortune, no Truth in their minds

People are in wanting

They have no place to rest in their minds

People just follow the false and end up in the false world

It is a life with no meaning, no value

When one builds false fortunes within his self

And accumulates false fortunes within his self

There is no meaning

The matters of life pass like wind and water

His life is difficult

Because he lives only for his greedy self

When one pursues only wealth and fame, his demons grow

There is no meaning; life is only full of falseness


Only a person who has Truth within the true mind

Will live eternally with that fortune, free of troubles

This is the best way of living

# Live As The True Shape

———

Fly

Rest

Run

Walk

Everything exists according to its own shape

Do not cry

Do not laugh

Just live

Live as it is

Live as your true shape

Live without mind, like nature

Abiding by nature

Like rain, wind, clouds, water and all creations

Live without mind, like nature


Do without the mind of doing

Have great mercy and compassion

Love truly

Live with true affection

Abiding by the flow of nature


Nature allows all creations to live

Through its fruits, its rewards

Likewise, just do as nature's flow,

Which is the greatest love in the universe

Just live that way


The true self dies when

One lives only for his self, for his body

One dies because he has no true self

So be your own true shape and live as your own true shape

The true shape is a non-material entity

Which exists but does not exist; which does not exist but exists

Non-material existence

Is great nature itself

And is Truth, which exists as it is

Without judgment or discernment

# Among The Ordinary There Is The Extraordinary

Just as there are no trees

In places that are too high

People who believe they are the greatest

Are like high mountains where trees cannot grow

For they have no one around them

One who has a large open mind without self

Can accept everything

One who is Truth without self

Achieves ultimate love and intimacy with people

He loves all

Has great mercy and compassion

And treats others with great love

With that great love

And without even the mind of having done so, he saves people

Accepting everything with the original mind

Without discernment or judgment

Everything lives within him

Among the ordinary there is the extraordinary

A distinguished person thinks only he is excellent and supreme

But the ordinary person can accept everything

With the greatest mind

And lives

With the extraordinary and remarkable wisdom of the Creator

He who lives in harmony

With the people in the world

With true love

Is the extraordinary one

But no one knows this man is extraordinary

One who enjoys being exalted

Cannot live in harmony for only he is excellent

He is the foolish one

For he lives with his own standards of

What is good and what is bad

An extraordinary person is one who is reborn as Truth

A foolish person is one who is not reborn as Truth

To live well means to be reborn as Truth and to live as Truth

To live poorly means to die

All is one

He who is liked by everyone

He who has no thorns, no ill will, in his mind

He who sees everything as it is

He who sees others just as they are even with all their faults

And he who has no mind of his self

Is the extraordinary one

Among the ordinary is the extraordinary

The ordinary is

The greatest, the most distinguished, and sublime perfection

But no one knows this

For there is no one who is truly ordinary

One who is ordinary can accept everything

For he has a large, open mind

# Completion Is To Accomplish All And To Be Fully Enlightened

Living silently like nature
Living silently like the universe
Is the life of Truth

Truth is the Great Soul and Spirit of the universe. He who has become Truth is one who has been reborn as the soul and spirit of Truth. The Creator is this Great Soul and Spirit. This is the only existence that is everlasting and never-dying. It is the energy and light of the universe itself. It is Truth; and one who is reborn as its body and mind has no death because it is Truth itself.

The Bible says that man does not live by bread alone but by the words of God. The word, logos, means rationality. The meaning of rationality is the fundamental nature of God. The word of God is the universe before the universe, which is the fundamental nature. That the universe was created by the word means Truth – the Creator, the fundamental nature – created the universe.

Truth is the universe before the universe, the Creator; it is the Great Soul and Spirit of the universe, which is indeed the Creator. It is the eternal, never-dying God. The minds of those who become God have no death and live eternally in the land of the never-dying God. Only God, the Great Soul and Spirit of the universe, created the universe and can make everything in it live. Humans think that they live by their own will. But what they do not know is that they live by God's will. The Great Soul and Spirit of the infinite universe first created the universe, and then made all creations exist. Soon after, there was a period when all creations and people multiplied on this land, for which there has been increase in population. Now is the time of harvest, when the Great Soul and Spirit of the universe allows more people to live eternally. This is the will of God. Only when God comes to this world as a human can humans achieve completion by becoming Truth, God. A human who has Truth can make humans become Truth. This is Truth.

All creations have yin and yang and they are the representations of God. One will live eternally without death when he is reborn as the origin, the God of yin and yang, the energy and light of the universe.

Only when there are beans can beans be created. Wheat brings wheat, rice brings rice, barley brings barley, cows bring cows, pigs bring pigs and humans bring humans. Likewise, only when there is a human with Truth can humans with Truth be born.

Mankind has been avidly pursuing Truth for a long time. There have been many stories about Truth, but these stories about Truth have been told based only on as much as the storyteller knows. A saint would have taught as much Truth as he knows. However, only the entity of Truth itself can make others become that existence of Truth. Humans cannot become Truth by themselves. Only when there is Truth, can people be reborn as Truth. If till now, there had been people who were Truth, then there should be a method on how to become Truth. It is likely that the reason why there has not been a method to become Truth until now, is because there was no one who had become Truth. People assume that there were many who had become Truth in the past. However, the question is, 'How much they had been enlightened?' and 'What had they realized through enlightenment?' A person who is reborn as the perfect Creator, Truth, must be one who is reborn as the soul and spirit of the universe one hundred percent.

A person who has God within, in other words, a person who has the Creator of the universe within, is born again as the mind of God and becomes one with the mind of the universe. The person who is reborn as the soul of the universe knows that material and non-material are one. Thus, his body itself is reborn as the body of Truth. The person whose mind is reborn as the soul and spirit of the universe is enlightened and knows that he is perfect; thus, his self has neither a past nor a future. He who is reborn as Truth, the soul and spirit of the Creator, the eternal never-dying God, lives as it is in the eternal never-dying kingdom of God. The individual is the soul and spirit of the whole. The whole is the soul and spirit of the individual. The individual and whole are the energy and light of the universe, which are one. Therefore, there is no death. What this tells us is that since Truth is the soul and spirit of the universe before the universe, we cannot live unless our bodies and minds are reborn as the body and mind of the universe. Only Truth can teach Truth and only Truth can create Truth. Now is the time to become Truth through human completion. When life and death are the same, one can live eternally.

This world is hell. When one discards mind and body from this world and discards the earth and the universe which is the kingdom of hell, then the unfading Truth is revealed and there will be the kingdom of Truth. Only he who has Truth and the kingdom of Truth in him will live eternally in the kingdom of Truth. He will live on as non-material shape, which is the soul and spirit of Truth.

# Death

Clouds float peacefully
In the infinite sky

People do not know the laws of the universe
People do not know the will of the universe

This universe exists and I exist
I am here by the harmony of the universe

Everything exists
Because of this and that, because of that and this
Yet, there is no one who knows it

People die in vain, because of the minds they have
Those who leave have no place to go
And live in hell, which is death
This is because people are not
In the right moment, at the right time, in the right season

# Only A Person Who Has Become Truth Lives

Amidst the eternity of time

The reason I came into this world as a human being

Is to live

Only the one who knows the will of the Creator

Knows the meaning of this

What are the unsatisfied desires you have?

What are you trying to gain, that you deny the will of God

And strive to be the best through your own will?

But is there anything you can achieve?

You do not know

What to have or what to accomplish in order to achieve

And you live not knowing

That you must become one with the Creator of the universe

A person who is born on earth lives on earth

A person who is born in heaven by becoming one with heaven

Lives in heaven

Humans do not know this

The dead remain dead unaware of this

Humans know neither life nor death

Not knowing what is important

They only look to feed the body

They are far from Truth

Living means that one who becomes Truth lives

Living means that one must be Truth in order to live

Living means that the kingdom of Truth must exist to live

Living means that the soul and spirit, which is life itself

Must exist to live

Life is the consciousness of that soul and spirit

A person whose consciousness is living will live and

A person whose consciousness is dead will die

A person whose consciousness is living

Is one who is God itself and the mind of God

He is one whose mind – the soul and spirit, Truth – is living

Therefore he is one who is alive

A person who is reborn as Truth

Which is the body and mind of the universe

Is one who is living

The person who is reborn as energy and light itself

As the origin of the universe while living

Will have

As much blessings as he accumulates in the kingdom of heaven

And live according to how much power he has in the kingdom

He will live forever with his blessings

People can live

Only according to what they have in their minds

A person whose mind is reborn as Truth has no death

Because his mind is Truth

A person whose mind

Is reborn as the soul and spirit, body and mind of Truth

Will live eternally without death

In the kingdom of Truth

One who is reborn as Truth

Is the Creator because he is the son of the Creator

People do not know that only Truth can deliver Truth

Although Truth is here in this world

No one knows Truth

Because people have their own minds of attachments

Only Truth can teach Truth

Only Truth can let people become Truth

Great nature is profound and mysterious

Because of this, that exists

Because of that, this exists

In the midst of everything in the universe

Many things come and go and many things change with time

These are nature's conditions

Wolves go where owls cry

Snakes go where there are frogs

Cats go where there are mice

Many things come and go, yet all return to great nature

And only the soul and spirit, body and mind of great nature

Remains as it is

Things come and go, go and come

Yet everything is that existence

All creations that come from the harmony of the earth

Live by their conditions

When the conditions are no longer there

Everything goes and no longer is

Existence is born because existence exists

The origin of that existence is

The soul and spirit of the great universe, which is one

People live and eventually their bodies die

But a person who is reborn

As the undying soul and spirit of Truth

Lives eternally without death in the universe

With that soul and spirit

The individual and the whole are one

Because there is only the whole itself

This is the whole

The individual is the whole itself

The whole, the body and mind of the universe,

And the energy and light,

Are one with the universe within the individual

Because the individual is reborn as Truth

It is the energy and light of the universe itself

That does not die

When a person becomes Truth

Whatever he sees, it is the Truth that is seeing

Whatever he hears, it is the Truth that is hearing

Truth itself sees and hears everything

The shape of Truth

Is that of humans and all creations

A person who has Truth, the universe, in his mind

Is energy and light (God) itself, Truth of heaven

Which is without death

Thus, from the perspective of Truth

The individual and the whole are one

Because he has Truth within

God is living but God just exists as it is

When the shape of each creation becomes God

It changes into the great mind of nature

And lives the life of nature

All is Truth and lives in the kingdom of Truth

However, humans cannot see or hear Truth

Because humans do not have it within their minds

Because humans have not been able to become it

By completely surrendering both body and mind

A person who becomes Truth has no death

As he is reborn as the mind and body of the universe

Everything in the kingdom of Truth

Will live because the individual and the whole are one

The person who becomes Truth while living

Has no death and can live eternally

# The Kingdom Of Light

The new kingdom

The new universe

The new world

The new mind

The new land and new heaven

The living world

The living kingdom

The living universe

The living mind

The living land and living heaven

The true world

The true kingdom

The true universe

The true mind

The true land and true heaven

# The Difference Between One Who Cleanses
# And One Who Has Accomplished

Come for me, come to see me

Come to me when you become me

Such is a person who has accomplished Truth

One who comes for his self is still cleansing

One who comes for me is completely cleansed

One who works for my kingdom is one who is cleansed

One who works for my kingdom has accomplished Truth

One who works for my kingdom accumulates blessings

One who works for my kingdom has the power of heaven

One who works for my kingdom

Accumulates heavenly blessings

One who works for my kingdom is Truth

One who works for my kingdom lives the life of nature's flow

One who works for my kingdom has wisdom

One who works for my kingdom has fully achieved Truth

One who works for my kingdom accumulates eternal blessings

One who works for my kingdom

Accumulates undying treasures

# The Master Is The Universe
# All Creations Are Also The Master

Mountains are high

Mountain waters run clear

Birds sing placidly

In the noisy city humans live

As if their nesting place were the city

Likewise mountains are the birds' nesting place

Each bird sings a strange tune

But each song is its words

Nature is thick with green

The forest is dense


Where does nature come from?

Everything lives according to its shape

Everything comes from the one soul and spirit

And goes to the one soul and spirit

Everything has its own life

All is new life itself

God and Buddha have already saved the world

This universe is already enlightened

This universe is already living

There is no death in the new world

There is no pain in the new world

There is no aging in the new world

There is no illness in the new world

Living eternally as it is in the new world


In the new world

Everything exists but it is not existence

All do not exist but it is not non-existence

Only Truth lives


The universe exists because

It exists from existence

It does not exist from non-existence

It seems as if nothing originally exists

It seems as if the universe does not exist

But the universe has always existed

And the universe is the master

If there are no clouds in the sky, only the sky is there

Even if there are clouds in the sky, the sky is still there

If there are no stars in the sky, the sky is there

Even if there are stars in the sky, the sky is still there

If there is no sun in the sky, the sky is there

Even if the sun is in the sky, the sky is still there

If there is no moon in the sky, the sky is there

Even if the moon is in the sky, the sky is still there

If there is no earth in the sky, the sky is there

Even if the earth is in the sky, the sky is still there

If there are no humans in the sky, the sky is there

Even if there are humans in the sky, the sky is still there

The sky created all creations

That sky is the mother and father of all creations

All creations are the offspring of the sky

All creations are the embodiment of the sky

All creations are the sky itself


This sky exists eternally

Both before and after the beginning


Only this sky itself lives eternally

This itself is Truth, energy and God itself


This is the never-changing Truth

It is the living existence, and therefore it is the Creator

The person who is reborn as this existence is a miracle

# Truth And Man Are Not Separate

Since long ago, the Korean people have searched for divinities of heaven and earth and searched for God. When a child was born, they prayed to what was called the 'Samshin Grandmother,' a divinity that governed childbirth. This 'Samshin Grandmother' was not only the goddess of childbirth, but also the creator of the shapes of all creations; she was Truth itself, the body of Buddha, the Holy Ghost, and the body of the universe. Thus, Koreans have lived with Truth and God since long ago.

From ancient times, 'Jungkamnok,' a book of prophecy written in the mid-Joseon Dynasty of Korea, prophesied not only the fate of our nation but also the precise time when everyone becomes Truth and when the world becomes Truth. This book states that through cleansing the mind, all become Buddha and go to the kingdom of heaven.

People think they live in this world doing whatever they want according to their own will. They do not know that God, the original existence, exists. They do not know that they live according to the plan and will of God. Because God is alive,

God can come as a person. This person is God. This person and God are completely one. Because God is Truth, God who has come in human form can teach humans to become Truth. Anyone who is reborn as God is God itself.

I have found that there are many who think that Truth and man are separate. When Truth comes as a human being, he can teach Truth and make people become Truth. People can never find Truth if they look for Truth in shapes or if they look outside themselves.

Although the universe, Truth, is silent, the existence of Truth who can make man Truth comes at a precise time. The most fortunate of the fortunate are those of us who are in the right season, at the right time.

# An Enlightened Person Is Silent

That an enlightened person is silent means

That a person who has become Truth and is complete

Has no judgment and discernment

His mind is

The greatest mind

When he becomes the mind of Truth

That is, when he is enlightened

He sees as it is and lives as it is

That is why he is silent

He sees everything as it is

That is why he is silent

# Enlightenment Is Believing, Living, Knowing All Scriptures, And Going To Eternal Heaven

Enlightenment comes only when you are Truth. Your mind is only as big as yourself. When your mind becomes as big as the universe before the infinite universe, you are enlightened. What one's self-centered false self believes in is the self-centered false God, Buddha, and Allah. This is not believing in Truth. For example, if I believe in God, and I merely say, "I believe, I believe," then is this true faith? You can believe in an existence only when your mind becomes that existence itself. Believing with your mind is true faith. This is enlightenment. The faith of those not enlightened is false belief. As your mind becomes Truth, you will gain enlightenment only as much as the Truth you come to have within. You believe as much as you have within you. That is because enlightenment comes only when you become Truth. What is true faith? Is it going to a place of worship often, praying often, singing and preaching well, or donating a lot? True faith is when you believe with your mind.

The mind controls actions and behaviors. Each person

has a different mind and thus acts accordingly. This is the reason why people are only able to speak of what they have learned. People have only stored and accumulated things in their minds, unable to throw away what they have in them. The body is the temple and sermon hall of God. When you cleanse what has been scribbled in that temple and cleanse the self, then you will have enlightenment according to how much Truth has been revealed to you. As Truth dwells in one's mind, this is faith. Only when one's mind believes and becomes that existence itself, is there faith. Faith is enlightenment; enlightenment is faith.

When you break your self-centered narrow mind, which is your sin, only then can you be Truth. Cleansing the self-centered mind means being absolved of your sins and freeing yourself from your karma. Complete absolution is the way to become one with Truth.

People speak and act according to what they have in their minds. There can be no Truth when you try to store the things you have heard about Truth within. Only when the self is no more, will there be Truth in your mind. One can only be as much Truth as his self has been discarded. This is being absolved of your sins, being free from karma; this is true faith.

A person who has Truth in his mind knows nature's flow and knows the Bible, sutras and all other scriptures. When you are absolved of your sins, when you are free from your karma, this land is heaven and you can live in this kingdom of heaven eternally, where life and death are the same; and you can do this while you are living. Just as you live according to what you have in your mind, only when you have Truth and the kingdom of Truth in your mind while you are alive, will there be no death. You have no death because you are the forever-living, never-dying God, which you can only become when you have Truth and the kingdom of Truth in your mind. Because you are born in heaven, you will live in heaven. It is illogical to say that a person who does not have heaven while living can go to heaven after death.

Changing your own fate can be achieved by changing your own mind. Having Truth in the mind is through the absolution of one's sins and the cleansing of one's karma. It is enlightenment and faith. You will be able to know the Bible and sutras through the absolution and cleansing of karma; through such absolution is the way to eternal heaven while living.

# When One's Consciousness Becomes That Of Truth

To have consciousness is to be aware. When we see a person who is dependent on an oxygen inhaler while in a coma, we say that he has lost his consciousness. Humans think they know how to live, but they live by their delusional knowledge according to what they have within. Humans communicate pursuant to their own thoughts, judgments, discernments and discriminations thinking that they are right. Such thinking occurs due to their self-centered point of view.

When your consciousness becomes that of the true consciousness, you are in the state of not-knowing. However despite this, you know what is righteous. It is the empty mind where there is an absence of knowing. Everything is emptiness itself. The shape of such a consciousness is that of the living consciousness of God, which is the size of the mind of the infinite universe. It is a state that transcends beyond 'clearness' or 'purity.' In the midst of where nothing exists, the sole God exists. He who is reborn as the mind of the sole God has the consciousness of God of wisdom itself. His consciousness does not belong to this or that; it is free, severed from all knowledge; it is emptiness itself. When excrements float down a clear river, you can see it easily. Likewise, one who is Truth can immediately distinguish one who lies, one who has a deceptive mind, one who says false words and one who has a false mind, from one who speaks Truth and one who is Truth. 'Doing without the mind of having done' means to just do because there is no mind of 'doing.'

The consciousness of Truth is wisdom itself. It is the consciousness that transcends beyond the word, 'consciousness.' It transcends to the point whereby when there is no false mind we can say, 'There is no consciousness.' The consciousness of Truth is living wisdom itself; it is Truth itself, which is free of vain false minds.

The consciousness is God itself. It is to know Truth. When you know everything, you will exist as it is, you will live as it is and you will be as it is. In this state there is no further enlightenment. The consciousness is God itself, and therefore, it is the forever-living existence, the state where there is no mind of living.

# The Living And The Dead

---

Generally when we speak of death, it is in reference to the life of the physical body ending. However, death of the mind, in other words, death of the soul and spirit, is different from this.

Our bodies are material, yet, what makes this material object move is the non-material mind. We act, speak and live according to what we have in our minds. For a person who has his own mind instead of Truth, he will live in hell when his body dies, a hell that does not exist, just like a dream. One whose mind is reborn as the eternal never-dying energy of the universe, God, has no death because he has Truth within. He lives with a true body and mind in the kingdom of the true body and mind. Existence and non-existence are not separate. They are the energy of the universe, and God itself. They are Truth itself. One whose body and mind are reborn as Truth is living. The dead knows neither the living nor the dead. But the living knows both the dead and the living.

One's thoughts arise according to what he has in his mind. One who has his thoughts is a person who has delusions and demons. He who believes that what he thinks is Truth, and that what he thinks is right must cleanse his delusional mind and body. Then when he is reborn in heaven while living and becomes Truth, he can live eternally.

A person knows that he is Truth and knows that he is living when he has become Truth. One who has not yet become Truth knows that he is not yet complete. One who has not become Truth, one who has not become complete, will die when his body dies. He will live in hell, in the kingdom of delusions, which does not exist.

# What Is True?
# What Is False?

One who has become Truth is true

One who has not become Truth is false

The age of the creation of the body and mind of the universe is

The age when only Truth lives

One who has become complete is living

One who has not become complete is dead

# What Is Maum Meditation?

Many people are curious about what Maum Meditation is. People generally say that other practices are quasi if it is not their own. But there must be something real in Maum Meditation because it flourishes with time. There must be something different because families and relatives practice together, and parents recommend this meditation to their children, and children to their parents, siblings to siblings, and friends to friends. Nowadays people are calculative and thus people would not come to practice Maum Meditation if there were no benefits in doing so. Therefore, people come to practice because there are indeed benefits in practicing Maum Meditation.

Maum Meditation teaches how to cleanse falseness – the pictures of past memories – which we have accumulated through our self-centered experiences. It teaches us that we are the biggest sinners and that our bodies and minds must be cleansed. Then it teaches us to cleanse the universe in our delusional minds so that we can know and become Truth. From start to finish, Maum Meditation is a place that focuses only on cleansing oneself. When one cleanses his self and everything in the universe, only the pure universe, Truth remains. Maum Meditation is the place, where one is reborn as the body and mind of the pure universe and goes to heaven where life and death are one; it is the place to deny and cleanse the self; it is the place to cleanse the self because you can only be reborn as Truth when you are cleansed.

To be quasi is when something is not real yet similar to the real thing. How can a place which allows one to become real be quasi? Is a place that only speaks of Truth quasi? What is false and quasi about cleansing oneself? Why must we argue over such a moot point?

We must become real now. Now it is the time for us to go to the forever-living heaven, the real world, while living. To become real is to become Truth, to reach completion while living.

When I have quasi notions in my mind I can see the quasi minds of others. It is because I am quasi that I see others as being quasi.

Everything is the shape of our own minds and karma.

Do not blame others and the world. When you reflect upon yourself, you will see how self-centered and hypocritical you really are. When you repent your self-centered and hypocritical self, you will be Truth, and there will be the kingdom of Truth.

Maum Meditation is the place to cleanse both body and mind to become Truth. As it is cleansed of falseness, your mind becomes clear and true, and thus, it becomes more comfortable. Because all illnesses are caused by the mind, there are many cases where people are cured from their illnesses and become healthier after practicing Maum Meditation. Maum Meditation exists in order to make human completion possible for everyone. Anyone can become a saint, know the flow of nature, and go to the forever-living heaven where life and death are one while living. Maum Meditation is the place where the ultimate purpose of mankind's existence can be achieved.

# What Is Wisdom?

When someone studies well, has a successful career, or deals with difficulties well, people think he is a wise man. However, such successes do not mean that one is wise. True wisdom is to know with the consciousness of God.

The Bible says that to know God is the foundation of wisdom. When a person's false mind is eliminated and he has the consciousness of God – the consciousness of Truth – he will have wisdom and know nature's law. That is to say that only God has wisdom. When one is reborn from the individual mind to the great mind of God, the mind of the whole, he has the wisdom to know the whole.

# We Must Be Reborn As The Holy Ghost

The universe consists of the Great Soul and Spirit itself. The Holy Ghost refers to the 'soul' of Truth. The word 'holy' is added to this soul, thus, creating the word 'Holy Ghost.' The original state of the Holy Ghost is where nothing exists. The Holy Ghost of the great universe brings forth all creations in the universe, and the physical forms of all creations are the embodiment of the Holy Ghost.

Because humans are sinners, their bodies and minds cannot become the soul and spirit of Truth. To be reborn as the soul and spirit of Truth through absolution of one's sin is to be reborn as the Holy Ghost.

The last phase of becoming Truth is to become Truth through absolution of one's sin and be reborn as the Holy Ghost. We must be reborn as the body and mind of Truth.

# What People Know

What people know is what they have selfishly stored in their minds from learning, seeing, and hearing in this self-centered world. Such is merely their subjective, self-centered knowledge. This is why in a world of six billion people there are six billion different minds.

If we ask people why we live and where we go, they will answer as much as they have learned but not be able to give a definite answer. Indeed, why do we live and where do we go? Those are the questions everyone is curious about but no one knows the answers to. The reason why man lives is to live forever, and those who live forever while living go to the living world, which is the kingdom of Truth.

What people know is what they have stored in their minds. When one has nothing in his mind and no longer has his body containing that mind, then Truth is revealed. Only when one is Truth will he truly know everything. To know everything is to be reborn in the kingdom of Truth and live there. One who knows everything is one who has become the living. Such a person accumulates his blessings in the kingdom of Truth by working in the kingdom of the living and saving the dead.

Humans do not know the nature of Truth because they do not have wisdom – God's consciousness – within their self-centered mind. That is why there is no one with wisdom.

# To Set Free

We can often see during celebrations around the world how birds are often set free to symbolize a new beginning. In Asia, fish are set free to streams and rivers.

For one to be free is to set free his self. It is to be reborn as Truth without self. When one becomes Truth it is freedom because his self no longer exists. When one becomes Truth he lives forever as it is. It is freedom, resurrection, eternal life, and heaven.

To truly be set free is to be free from the self and live as Truth.

# Do Not Be Loyal To Your Body Which Will Rot Away

People want to be comfortable, eat well, live affluently and live long lives without illness. They want to spare their bodies, and they do not want to do difficult work or do work that others do not want to do. They want their children to be successful and to take care of them when they become old, when they become ill, or when they are close to death. A few decades ago it was difficult to live past sixty, but now our lifestyles have improved and it is common to live past seventy or even eighty. So as people live a mere seventy or eighty year, they live their lives only for their false bodies. But no matter who you are, our bodies will eventually die, rot and become soil.

The best way to live with wisdom is to be reborn with the body and mind of Truth now and live in the kingdom of Truth. In the Bible, it says that the foolish accumulate treasures on the earth and the wise accumulate treasures in heaven. To be reborn as the mind and body of Truth and to live in the kingdom of Truth is to accumulate treasures in the kingdom of Truth within oneself, and those treasures become his forever.

There is nothing more precious than this. Rather than seeking good clothes, good food, and comfort for the false body, the wise will become Truth and accumulate their treasures by working in the kingdom of Truth. Do not build your own kingdom for the false body that will die and rot away. Instead, even if we were to live only for a day, let us accumulate our blessings in our minds, the kingdom of Truth, by devoting our bodies.

People in the past spoke about life's futility. Those who recited words and poems of futility have all passed away. Likewise, we too will pass on after seventy or eighty years of life. However, even though our bodies are no more, those who can go to the forever-living land, those who have a place to return to, and those who are already there must have their true blessings in this true land in order to live eternally in that land with their own blessings.

# You Can Only Go To Heaven And Live Forever Without Life And Death While You Are Living
## You Cannot Go There After Death

People do not have wisdom – they do not know what is righteous, what is Truth. Ask yourself whether you are Truth, whether you are a complete person. I have asked numerous people this same question. I have not met anyone who could say 'I am Truth.' This means that his false self has admitted that he is false; he has admitted that he is not complete.

Completion is without want

Completion is to be forever without death

Completion is to accomplish all

Completion is to live forever

Only Truth, the Creator, is complete

Completion is the eternal never-dying body and mind

Completion is to have all

Completion is to become Truth itself

Heaven, the kingdom of Truth, is the kingdom where only the complete, only those who are reborn as Truth, live. This kingdom is the universe before the universe, which is the father and mother of all creation; it is the universe before creation.

This kingdom is the Great Soul and Spirit itself, which existed before the beginning and will exist beyond eternity. It is the never-dying body and mind, an existence that exists on its own. It is the self-existing, everlasting entity. This existence is omnipresent but cannot be seen by human eyes. Even though it is living, people cannot see this existence because it does not exist within their minds. Since people live believing that what they have learned, seen, heard and experienced is who they are, they do not have this existence of Truth, and therefore it does not exist within their minds.

When one's mind becomes the mind of the infinite universe by cleansing his false self, he will have the Creator within him and he can see Truth, the Creator; he can be reborn as the child of Truth. The way to go to heaven is to cleanse one's mind, even one's self, and to cleanse the universe he has in his false mind, for which there remains an existence that never disappears no matter how hard one tries to eliminate it. This existence is Truth and the kingdom of Truth. When one does not exist and his mind is reborn as the child of Truth, as the Great Soul and Spirit of Truth, that is when he is complete, has accomplished all, and has become Truth. Only Truth can live in the kingdom of Truth.

If you do not become Truth while living, and if you do not become real while living, then you will indeed die since you are false. Only the real will live because he is Truth. Only a person who is real can live in the real land. Does it make sense that one who has not become real while living can go to heaven after death? One who is false, in other words, one who is not real, will die because he is not Truth. He will suffer the pain of hell in his mind. A person who becomes Truth while living is one who has the living kingdom of Truth; he will live in that kingdom. Only a person who is real now can live in the real kingdom. There is nothing more perfect, more supreme or greater in the world than Truth. By repenting, we must go to heaven now while living. Some religions say their leaders can take them to heaven. Other religions say that certain beings will bring only the faithful to heaven. One who has faith is one who is enlightened of Truth and has Truth within through absolution of his sins. How can one go to heaven without believing in and becoming Truth? Needless to say, one who is not Truth now, one who is not complete now, cannot go to heaven, the kingdom of Truth.

# One Who Is Completely Enlightened
# One Who Has Accomplished All
# One Who Knows All

Complete enlightenment, complete achievement, and complete wisdom are different terms, but they all have the same meaning. Enlightenment of Truth is relative according to how much one's mind is cleansed. However, complete enlightenment, complete accomplishment, and complete wisdom is to be born again and live in heaven, the kingdom of Truth.

When you are reborn and live in heaven you are completely enlightened, you accomplish all, and you come to know all. As you go from the dark kingdom to the kingdom of living light, you will be enlightened, be accomplished and know everything. Being reborn and living in that kingdom is to completely be enlightened, to accomplish all, and to know all.

# The Living World

Blue birds are blue

Sparrows are sparrow-colored

Each is camouflaged in its own way

Other animals also have their own colors for protection

Each creation lives, dies and is born in a specific way

Nobody taught it how to breed and nurture

Yet it breeds and nurtures, comes and goes on its own

Just as Truth exists on its own

Everything on this earth lives a limited life then goes away

One who does not know where to go

One who does not have a place to go grieves

But one who knows where to go

One who knows there is no going and coming

Remains as it is

One must carve out his own destiny

Furthermore human completion can

Only be achieved by one's utmost efforts

While nature's principle is

That each creation exists on its own

There is still cause and effect

While nature's principle is

That every creation exists through the harmony of this and that

The origin of all is one

All shapes are the manifestation of the origin

The shapes of all things living are the life of the origin

The whole of creation is already living and enlightened

This land is already heaven, however

Only people, as they are not enlightened

Are trapped and dead in their tombs

Those whose consciousnesses are not reborn as that of Truth

Are dead

Those who are not the undying energy of the universe

The original soul and spirit itself

Are dead

Every creation on this earth that is in the kingdom of God

Is living

But because people do not know God

Because they have not become one with God

People live in the kingdom of the dead; they live in hell

People live according to what they have in their mind

Therefore one who has

The eternal and never-dying God in his mind

Will live as it is without death

People live busily earning money

However, the more palaces you build

In your body that will eventually die away

The harder it is to come out from your deep grave

You are merely digging

A deeper, more fortified tomb of death for yourself

One who lives as Truth and does things as Truth

One who has accumulated his fortunes in the kingdom of Truth

Will live eternally with that fortune

Such is a wise man

The existence or non-existence of all creation depends on

Whether it exists or does not exist in a person's mind

He who has Truth in his mind

Knows that all is one and that all is living

He lives as it is, and exists as it is, eternally, forever and ever

Like wind, like water, without hindrance

By the will of the universe

# The Master

Though I exist in the clouds no one has seen me

Though I exist in the wind no one has seen me

Though I exist in the universe no one has seen me

Though I exist in the world no one has seen me

Though I exist within people no one has seen me

No one has seen me because they do not have the universe


The reason why people cannot live is

Because they do not have the origin, God of life, in their minds

The universe exists as it is

While Humans pass through this world

As mere wanderers


When you become the owner, the master

You will have the entire universe

When you become one

With the origin of existence and non-existence

You will have everything in the universe

You will have the universe within you

And you will live forever and ever

In the kingdom of life without death


Human completion is when

One's soul and spirit is reborn

As the soul and spirit of the universe

To live is when

Both existence and non-existence

Become life itself

To live is when

The human mind is reborn

As energy of Truth and God, the soul and spirit

To live is to become Truth

By surrendering all of one's individual self

Until only Truth remains


To live is one

To live is Truth

To live is to be the master

To live is to be the forever-living, never-dying master

# People Mistake Themselves As Buddha

We have heard many times that we are Buddha. The whole of creation in the universe is already enlightened; the kingdom of God or Buddha is already completed and every creation is alive. But, because of their false minds, people are dead and trapped in their own graves. Because of their minds, which are evil, people live as slaves to their minds. When you cleanse the self which is evil, and are reborn as Truth – the living Great Soul and Spirit – only then are you Buddha. Buddha is the existence of Truth; Buddha is the soul and spirit, the Creator, the universe before the universe. Sin and karma are false, for which total absolution of such sin and karma is for the self to disappear. One can be Buddha not by having Buddha in himself but only when he is reborn as Buddha. Some people cannot finish this meditation because they still have an egotistical frame of mind and try to put Buddha within themselves. Such people are those whose karma is heavy, who are sinful. For those who have a lot of karma, it is difficult to become Buddha. When one is reborn as Buddha without his self, he is Buddha.

# The Absurd Seeking Heaven In Shapes And In The Material World

The master of the universe, the kingdom of energy and light, is Truth. When the human mind becomes the master of the universe, this is when the universe exists in that mind. All creations live by the master's mind and all creations are the master. Humans have eternal heaven in their minds, yet absurdly they do not seek from within; instead they wait and expect for an alien UFO or some being to take them to a material heaven.

Such people read scriptures from their own viewpoint, misinterpreting the words. They do not understand the metaphors of the scriptures so they cannot correctly interpret the meaning. In the Sutras, it says Buddha and heaven are in the mind; in the Bible, it says God, Truth, and heaven are in the mind.

A person's actions are governed by what he knows and what he has in his mind. People do not know the kingdom of Truth because they do not have the true world, the world of the true soul and spirit, the non-material world. People have their own false worlds because they do not have the kingdom of Truth. They do not know that their world is false. The material world and non-material world are not two, but one. Because people see only what they are able to see, they do not know the master, the origin, the non-material real existence, which cannot be seen. When people's minds are reborn from this existence, there is eternal life and heaven. To be reborn means to cleanse themselves and to be reborn as the soul and spirit, body and mind of this existence. Because people's minds do not have this existence within, they cannot see nor hear it. Therefore people have imagined and made presumptions about this existence for many years, but to no avail. This is because no one can know what it is unless they become this existence. Unless they reach this state, no one can know. People whose minds do not reach this state will never understand.

You will know Truth, as much as you have reached the state of Truth, as much as your mind becomes Truth. One can never know about a state he has not reached. One who does not have Truth cannot know while one who does can because people know only as much as they have within their minds. You can only be reborn as Truth from the existence of Truth itself by cleansing the mind. You cannot be reborn if you hold on to your self. You can come to know about the land of the dead only when your body dies; and likewise, only when your self no longer exists will you be reborn as Truth. Truth is non-material existence. Only when Truth becomes one's self, will he be reborn and live.

# The River Is Silent

Rivers flow silently

In the past and in the present

All the people of the past have gone

And new people have come

Even though everything in the universe continuously changes

What never changes forever is the universe

The universe existed before eternity

And will exist after eternity

That is the only Truth there is

One who has that which is real within him is real

He is Truth

He will live as it is without death

Amidst the innumerable desires of human beings

They think they have everything

But there is no one who has Truth

Instead humans have useless false minds

And no one knows that his mind is false

All creations live when

One is reborn in the kingdom that is one

He will live in the kingdom of oneness forever

Do not live without knowing the meaning and reason of

What you live for, why you live, and where you go

Instead, when you live in Truth

Anyone can know the ways of the world

And live as the master of the world

Whether you know or not

Depends on

Whether you have Truth or falseness in your mind

Whether your mind is big or small

And whether your mind is clean or dirty

The true mind is the soul and spirit of the universe

It is purity itself

That transcends beyond the words 'clean' and 'clear'

The birth and death of humans

Existence and non-existence of humans

All are nature's flow; it is logic and reason

In the kingdom where all existence lives

All is living and 'I' am living

This kingdom is the complete heaven

When humans awake from their dreams and are reborn

They will know what it feels like to be awake

They will understand the mind of an awakened person

In their dreams humans do not know what is what

For they have no choice

But to dream what is written in the script of their dreams

# One Who Is Accomplished

He who is accomplished

Is one who has reached human completion

He who is accomplished

Is one who has become Truth

He who is accomplished is one who has become

The forever-living, never-dying soul and spirit

Knowing everything means

To be reborn in the kingdom of Truth

And to live the life of Truth

This is to know everything


Human completion is

To be reborn as Truth and

To live in the kingdom of Truth

He who has reached human completion is one who is complete

He who is complete while living

He who is reborn in the eternal heaven while living

Will live in that kingdom even after his body dies

# Who Will Accuse Whom?
# Who Will Blame Whom?

---

Only a wise person knows when he is to blame.

People easily blame their ancestors and others whenever things do not work out their way. Politicians also insist that they are right. This is why governments battle. Religions also insist that only theirs is right and that others are wrong, and so there has never been a time without religious conflict. Historically, people believe that religions which have become well-established over time are not false and that new religions are. This causes conflict. He who is not complete is false, so we must not make judgments of other religions or slander others, but rather just cleanse our false selves.

# Enlightenment

One must be enlightened in order to believe

One must be enlightened in order to live

One must be enlightened in order to understand every scripture

One must be enlightened in order to go to eternal heaven

# Light

When there is light

People who are asleep do not know it is daylight

Likewise when the world of light comes

People who are not in the world of light

Will not know it

Just as the universe exists according to one's mind

The universe is different according to one's mind

Some say they like it when it rains

While others say they do not

There are millions of different ways of seeing in the world

Depending on what one has in his mind

The world is already enlightened and perfect

However

The human mind is unable to become the enlightened world

Therefore

People see the world with their own fixed beliefs and habits

The state of the universe before creation is that of the Creator

The state of the universe before creation is the state of Truth

People know only what they have in their minds

People speak only of what they have in their minds

People can only become what they have in their minds

Likewise, Truth can be recognized

Only when their mind is clean and the greatest


A person with a false mind

Does not know that his mind is false

Only a person with Truth can recognize

The person whose mind is false

A crazy person does not know he is crazy

An ignorant person does not know his ignorance

Truth has no discernment or judgment for it knows everything

But people live making judgments on what is right and wrong

These judgments are one's own viewpoint

From one's own mind


The reason why the world is not one

Is because

Each person has different conceptions and different minds

All religions can become one

Only through absolution of sin

Only through becoming Truth

All countries can become one

Only when all minds are one through becoming Truth


Only Truth can make the world one

Only Truth can save the world

Only Truth exists forever and ever

One who is living is one who is reborn as Truth


One who is reborn in heaven while living

Will live in heaven, the living kingdom

One cannot go to eternal heaven

Without becoming Truth

Becoming Truth is the completion of humans, while living

# One Receives Divine Blessings Only Through Absolution Of One's Sins

We say we have received a blessing when someone helps us materially or spiritually. However, a true blessing is the blessing of Truth. The blessing of Truth is to be born again as Truth – the Creator, the holy soul and holy spirit – from the mind which is trapped in one's self. Then one has the true soul and spirit, and therefore, there is no death.

In Buddhism, the trinity means that the Sambhogakaya (body of Buddha), the Dharmakaya (mind of Buddha), and the Nirmanakaya (incarnation of Buddha) are one, as Buddha itself. In Christianity, the Holy Ghost, the Holy Father, and the Holy Son are one, as God. In Buddhism, the original existence is referred to as Buddha. Buddha is the holy soul and spirit, Truth. The holy soul and spirit is the body and mind of Buddha. Buddha, which is the origin, is the Creator. Every creation is the child of Buddha and the incarnation of the body and mind of Buddha. Likewise the Holy Ghost, Holy Father and Holy Son in Christianity have the same meaning, for which the Holy Ghost and Holy Father is the Creator and all creations in the universe are the children of this Creator. Humans, as well as all creations, were originally born as the children of this Creator, Truth. But humans were not able to become one with this existence because of their own conceptions of 'good and evil,' and 'right and wrong.'

The way to become one with this existence is by being absolved of one's sins through repentance. Sin consists of personal sin, which is the individual mind, and original sin, which is sin inherited from our ancestors upon birth. Our ancestors were also sinners and we are born with their shape. The mind of all creations and humans come from their own shapes wherein each individual has a different mind because they are of different shapes. When one cleanses his personal sin and original sin through repentance, he will be absolved from his sins. When one becomes free from his self-centered conceptions and behaviors which is his self-centered mind, he will have blessings by becoming Truth through absolution of one's sins.

When you are reborn as the body and mind of Buddha, as the soul and spirit of Truth, you will have the blessings of the Holy Ghost and Holy Father. You will know your blessings through enlightenment depending on how much of the Holy Ghost and Holy Father you have in your mind. To receive blessings through prayer means Truth is within you according to how much your mind is cleansed.

To receive true blessings means for one to no longer exist and be born again as the Holy Ghost and Holy Father. You will have true blessings when your soul and spirit is reborn as the living existence, the Creator, by cleansing the body and mind of your self.

# Resurrection

Resurrection is to be born again as the soul and spirit of the original, eternal, never-changing Truth by cleansing one's mind – the proud, unclean mind which is sin – as well as his body. When you are reborn as the body and mind of Truth, you are Truth; and you will live forever without death because you are a living existence.

Resurrection is to be reborn as the body and mind of the universe and to be reborn as Truth. The forever-living heaven is the world where only those who have been resurrected live. Only those who are resurrected while living go to the forever-living heaven. This kingdom is where a person can go when he has become Truth while living.

# Truth Is Universally Valid, Not Magic

The original Truth is

The universe before the universe

The soul and spirit of that place

Which exists where nothing exists

This is the original Truth

This existence is both the body and mind of the universe

The soul and spirit

Both the body and mind of Buddha

The Holy Ghost and Holy Father

All these are Truth

All creations are the children of such Truth


There are mountains in the world

There is water in the sea

There is fire

There are numerous kinds of trees

There are numerous kinds of plants

There are insects and reptiles

There are birds and fish

There are four-legged animals

There are humans, walking on two legs

There are many different creations

These countless shapes

Are all alive in the kingdom of Truth

All are living because they are the children of Truth

Therefore the world is already enlightened and

The kingdom of Truth is completed


When the Creator created this world

It was created in such a way that

Existence is co-dependent on each other

For which this must exist for that to exist and vice versa

Every creation comes forth on its own according to condition

All creations live life according to their shape

All creations act and live according to their shape

All creations live as they are and as you see them

Birds fly and fish live in the water

Animals crawl

People walk and run with two legs

No human flies

Everything living in this world

Is Truth just as you see it

However people try to seek Truth in miracles

The shapes of all creations is Truth

Living as it is and as you see it is Truth

People who seek Truth from miracles

Will never find the miracle they want

Because people misunderstand

The meaning of omniscience and omnipotence

They wait for a false truth

They expect the appearance of a false existence

However Truth is as you see it and as you hear it

Truth is as it is

# The Way To Heaven

Guiding people to heaven means to send both the dead and the living to the kingdom of Truth. People usually think that the way to guide a person to heaven is only possible after that person is dead. However, to truly guide people to heaven is to send both the dead and the living to heaven.

Maum Meditation guides the soul and spirit of the living to become Truth. It allows for one to be born in heaven while living. So if Maum Meditation can guide the living to heaven, it is needless to say that Maum Meditation can guide the dead to heaven as well. The way for the dead to enter heaven is the same as for the living. The souls and spirits of both a living person and a dead person are dead within their self-centered false world of attachments because of their sins and karma. Maum Meditation guides one's dead soul and spirit to cleanse his self-centered false world and to cleanse his false body and mind, which is hell. Then only Truth remains and the soul and spirit becomes Truth.

To guide a living person is to let him be reborn in

heaven by cleansing his self and his false world. To guide a dead person is to let him be reborn as Truth and live in heaven by cleansing his soul and spirit of his false world. Only the master of heaven is capable of delivering them unto heaven. When one owns something he can do as he pleases. It is the same for sending the living to heaven. In order for one to take others to heaven he must have heaven himself and have the method to take them to heaven. It does not make sense for someone to claim he can take others to heaven when he does not have a place to take them to.

Many people ask me what is the difference between people who live in heaven by practicing Maum Meditation and people who have been sent to heaven after they die. Those who live in heaven by practicing Maum Meditation live there with their blessings in heaven, which they accumulated while living. It is the same as stated in the Bible that the foolish accumulates his fortune on earth, and the wise accumulates his fortune in heaven. One who has become Truth will love Truth and the kingdom of Truth more than his family. There is nothing more important than being reborn as Truth and working in the kingdom of Truth while living because you will live forever with the blessings you have accumulated in the kingdom. Your treasures will be there forever and there will be as much blessings as you have accumulated. When you send material existence of your false world to heaven, the kingdom of Truth, that existence will be yours forever. That is how you accumulate your fortunes which you will live with forever. When you work in the kingdom of Truth and take what is yours to heaven, you will live eternally in heaven with your blessings.

# Enlightenment Comes Only When You Become Truth

When one cleanses his self-centered conceptions and behaviors, his mind becomes the existence of Truth. Then one will know Truth to the extent his mind has become cleansed and widened. He will know Truth according to how much he has become Truth. This is enlightenment.

Since youth, we have heard a lot about Truth from our parents and through various religions. However, no matter how much we have heard about Truth, we could not become Truth. Truth exists only when we cleanse our minds. This is why no matter how many stories of Truth we store in our minds we cannot become Truth.

Throughout life we unconsciously accumulate self-centered conceptions and behaviors while we see and hear numerous things. Then we live as slaves to these conceptions and behaviors, as our bodies follow our false minds. When my mind thinks of meeting someone, my body follows. When my mind decides to do this or that, then my body follows. When my mind decides to meet friends or go to the bathroom, then my body follows. Therefore, the master that makes the body move is the mind. People can live only according to what they have in their minds.

One can be reborn as Truth by cleansing the mind. Cleansing the shadows of numerous past memories and denying the existence of the self is the way to Truth. The way to Truth is to cleanse one's delusional conceptions and to deny the self's existence.

The existence of Truth is the one Great Soul and Spirit of the infinite universe. Enlightenment is knowing to the extent that my mind becomes this existence. There is no enlightenment in that which is not Truth, or that which is not heading towards Truth, because the mind stays within one's own frame. If one insists that something which is not Truth is Truth, he will have no enlightenment and no eternal heaven. Only when one heads towards Truth will there be enlightenment. Only when one is reborn as the soul and spirit of the infinite universe will he live because he is Truth. If someone thinks that an existence which is not Truth is Truth, then only when that existence is discarded will Truth appear. Truth cannot be discarded no matter how hard one may try.

One who sees that the Great Soul and Spirit is living and only one who is reborn as Truth, knows Truth. However, one who does not see the silent universe before the universe, which is Truth, thinks that putting any existence in the place of Truth will make that existence Truth. When one puts the existence which is not Truth in the place of Truth, then there is no more enlightenment; there is only death without eternal heaven. Only when one becomes the existence of Truth will there be enlightenment and eternal heaven.

# You Will Not Know What You Have Not Realized Because Your Mind Is Unable To Accept

For the past ten years I have spoken of Truth. What I said ten years ago and what I say now about Truth is the same. Those who heard my words back then say that it is only now that they can actually hear and understand what I have been saying.

People cannot understand the sutras, the Bible, or other holy scriptures if their level of enlightenment is not the same as those writings. They do not have Truth within their minds so they cannot hear even though they have ears; they cannot see even though they have eyes. This is because they are trapped in their self-centered conceptions and behaviors. People speak, know, and live according to what they have in their minds, and therefore those who do not have Truth in their minds do not know Truth. People cannot understand that which is slightly beyond the level of enlightenment they have achieved. No matter how hard I try to make them understand it is impossible because they do not have Truth in their minds.

Each level of Maum Meditation has a different level of enlightenment. In the first and second level we cleanse the mind.

First Level: Knowing I am the universe

Second Level: The universe and I are not separate because there is no mind

In the third and fourth level we cleanse the body.

Third Level: Realizing through enlightenment that the universe is in me

Fourth Level: Seeing and knowing the soul and spirit of the universe

Fifth Level: Knowing the soul and spirit of the universe is the master, Truth

Sixth Level: Knowing that here is heaven

Seventh Level: Being reborn as the body and mind, soul and spirit of the universe, by cleansing the self who knows Truth.

When you are reborn with the mind of the universe you are enlightened of the fact that your body is perfect, and you will live forever in heaven. In other words, this world is the world of Buddha and heaven while you are living, so the body and mind which are reborn as Truth in this world will live as the forever-living, never-dying God. Only one who becomes Truth and is reborn in heaven will live because he is Truth.

When I speak to Maum Meditation practitioners about Truth, I notice that they cannot understand that which is beyond their level of enlightenment. Many of them stop doing the meditation because they are not able to overcome their self-centered mind of conceptions and discernments.

It is only one's own mind that stops him. This is because he is trapped in his sin and karma. But despite everything, once he cleanses his self and his mind becomes bigger as he becomes Truth, he will come to know Truth.

The reason why one is unable to be enlightened is because he does not have a clean and big mind due to his conceptions and behaviors. And thus, he is unable to accept Truth.

# There Is Nothing Above Truth
# There Is Nothing Greater Than Truth
# That Which Is Not In The Kingdom Of Truth
# Is Hell, False, Delusional

In order for humans to accomplish completion and live forever, they must be reborn as the body and mind of Truth, which is what created the living universe. Truth is the highest existence and the existence that lives forever. It never changes and is the non-material real existence, which existed before and will exist after the beginning. Truth cannot be seen by human eyes. It can only be seen when it is in the human mind. Truth does not have a shape but all creations are the embodiment of this existence, for which it is the mother and father of all creation because everything comes from this. Truth never disappears even if we were to try endlessly to destroy or burn it. It is the perfect existence, which is self-existing and exists as it is. There is nothing greater than Truth, nothing beyond Truth, and only Truth is perfect. Nothing exists where Truth is and even this nothingness does not exist, yet God exists within this emptiness. This emptiness is the body of Truth; and God is the mind of Truth. Everything is born from this existence and everything is living because the body and mind of this existence is divine. Only this existence is perfect. The kingdom of this existence is a forever-living kingdom where life and death are one and the same; it is heaven. Only when the mind, which is one's consciousness, is reborn as this most perfect existence, can he live because he is Truth. If one does not become this existence, he will die. When one is reborn with the body and mind of Truth he will become a child of God, not a child of man.

In the quest for Truth, many have searched high and low and led an ascetic life in many different religions. However, no one has become complete. Humans are incapable of becoming complete on their own. If there were a person who had become complete, then a method to reach completion should already exist. There has been no such method in this world. It is common sense that the method to become Truth can only be given by the existence that is Truth itself. There was once an age of creation and an age of growth. Now is the age of completion. People are born in this period in order to become complete and to live eternally in the kingdom of completion. Some religions fantasize that the complete being of the past will return in the same shape as before. Other religions dream of the day when their founder will return. However, if becoming complete is Truth, then only a place that is Truth enables one to become complete.

Although Jesus came two-thousand years ago, the Jewish people are still waiting for their Messiah because they believe in the Old Testament to which they are bound. Similarly, when Truth does come, people will not recognize the Messiah, the second coming of Christ or Buddha, because they are bound to their own preconceptions. The truth that people wait for is a truth of human conception, because they try to find Truth in what they see.

In the Bible it states that Truth will come in a cloud. Maybe this means that when Truth comes, it cannot be seen by people because of the cloud. The cloud probably means the coming of Truth in human form. Nobody will recognize it; it comes like a thief. It is also said that nobody knows the time or day of the coming of the true existence except for the Father, God. It is obvious that if the true existence comes into this world then only the true existence itself will know. People will not know the true existence because they do not have Truth within. People only draw upon a person's appearance and life that they know, just as people only looked at Jesus' appearance and saw him merely as the son of a carpenter.

Only those who become Truth will know Truth while those who do not become Truth will never know it. Only the living can see the living; only Truth can see Truth. Truth cannot be seen by human eyes. People cannot see Truth. This means that humans cannot see or know Truth when it comes in human form. So all in all, is it common sense for the dead to come back to life? If so, then it is not Truth. Truth is as you see it and as it is according to nature's flow. If some existence asks you to go to his kingdom, then that kingdom is not the kingdom of Truth but hell; it is a delusional world.

Eternal life is living, without life or death. Only he who becomes Truth while living can go to the kingdom of Truth. Heaven is the kingdom where Truth itself, the never-dying God, lives. One cannot live in this kingdom unless one becomes Truth while living. To become Truth is to be saved and to live. To become Truth is resurrection, and to go to the eternally living heaven where life and death are one. It is for man to be reborn as the son of God. The ultimate purpose of humans to be born into this world is to reach completion and live forever.

# One Can Teach Only What He Has And That Is All That Can Be Learned From Him

What people know is what they have stored in their mind by seeing, hearing and learning throughout their life experiences. If we were to ask a person to speak Hindi, or talk about Hinduism, he would not be able to do so if he has not learned the language or experienced the religion. One does not know what one does not have. Likewise, no one knows Truth because Truth does not exist in their minds.

In this world, there are places where Truth is spoken about, such as in religious organizations or other groups, but there is no place where one can be made Truth. If there were such a place then the world would have become one, all religions would have become one, countries would have become one, and ideologies would have become one.

Only when the existence of Truth comes is it possible to make humans Truth. If there is no Truth in this world, no one will ever become Truth. Only the existence of Truth can make Truth because only it has Truth. Only Truth knows Truth and can make humans Truth. People do not know beyond what they have within. If people do not have Truth within they cannot know Truth, nor can they make others Truth.

People have religions, philosophies and ideologies of the world in their minds. People have numerous minds of the delusional false shadows of their life's past. People just keep putting all this in their minds without taking them out. The way to become Truth is by cleansing the delusional false mind and by being reborn as Truth. This is the only way to be reborn as the forever-living, never-dying existence, as the child of God.

There must be Truth in order for Truth to be born. Just as a person can teach only what he has, Maum Meditation has the method to become Truth. And thus Maum Meditation is the place where people can become Truth.

# Truth, God, Divinity, Buddha, The Creator, Allah
## All Are The True Existence

We have continuously heard about Truth, God, Divinity, Buddha, the Creator, Allah, but there does not seem to be anybody who truly knows them. Different names have been given to the existence of Truth depending on the region.

There is no existence greater than the existence of Truth and only this existence is omniscient, omnipotent, and perfect. It is the living existence without death. This existence created the material universe and only this existence is capable of spiritually waking the universe. It is the self-existing light and energy of the universe, the true existence. This existence is the body and mind of the universe; it is the universe before the universe, the sky before the sky, the place before the material existence and the place of the soul and spirit. In Korea, people have called this place Haneolim, which is Jung and Shin. Christians call this place God, which is the Holy Father and Holy Ghost. In Buddhism it is called Buddha, which is Dharmakaya and Sambhogakaya. Even though the names are different, they all refer the same existence – Truth.

The body and mind of Truth are two yet they are one existence. Only when one is reborn as the body and mind of this existence will he be reborn as the child of Truth. The mind of Buddha, the body of Buddha and the incarnation of Buddha are one. The Holy Ghost, Holy Father and Holy Son are one. All are one, and all are the world of Truth, which is heaven. Heaven is already enlightened and complete. Everything in heaven is living. Heaven is the world of the Holy Trinity. People must get rid of their karma and sin and be reborn as this existence and go to the kingdom of this existence.

When there are no clouds in the sky, only the sky remains
Even when there are clouds in the sky, the sky is still there

When there are no stars, no sun, no moon and no earth in the sky
Then only the sky remains
Even when there are stars, the sun, the moon, and the earth in the sky, the sky is still there

When there are neither humans nor everything in the universe

Then only the sky remains

Even when there are humans and everything in the universe

The sky is still there

This sky is the self-existing Creator, Truth, which existed forever before and exists forever after. This existence has been named differently depending on the region.

# What Is The New World?
# What Is The New Heaven And New Earth?
# Where Are They?

When people hear the words, 'new world,' 'new heaven,' and 'new earth,' they think that such a world will be created someday. They also think that these places exist somewhere else. It seems people are waiting for a new world because their lives are painful and troubled, or because they want the present world to disappear. They have these fantasies because the existing world does not fit in to the conceptions of their mind. In their conceptions, people have a mind only as big as their body due to greed. People do not know about the existence of the new world, the new heaven, and the new earth because they do not have the new world, the new heaven, and the new earth in their minds.

Only those of us whose minds become the body and mind of the universe before the universe, the Creator and our original master, can have the new heaven and new earth, which is the new world. Only when we have the widest, the largest, the lowest, and the highest mind, and only when the original Creator remains in our mind, do we have eternal life without life or death. Because the new heaven and new earth is in us, because Truth, the original place of pure energy and light is in us, the whole universe is the world of energy and light. It is God's kingdom. Only one who is reborn as this living existence will have within him the new world, the new heaven, and the new earth.

One whose mind becomes the world
And whose mind is as big as the world
Knows the laws of the universe
Knows the will of the universe
Because man has a mind that is
Limited to the size and shape of his body
He speaks only of himself
From his narrow mind of preconceptions
Not knowing that what he says is daft
Not knowing that what he says is dead and not true
The new world is a living world
When one is in it
Everything one speaks or does is Truth, is living
They are words of Truth and deeds of Truth

# The Difference Between What Is True And What Is False

When the mind is

The cleanest

The widest and the largest

The lowest and the highest

It is true

Falseness is to be a slave

In one's mind

To his mind as big as his shape

To the extent of how much he has learned

Which is not real

# Wanderer

Wanderer, do not wander about

Without knowing where to go

Find your way and find your resting place

Know that the place to rest is not outside but inside you


Even if the whole universe disappears

The eternal resting place remains as it is and is alive

If you want to know this

Cleanse yourself and be reborn in the kingdom of Truth

This kingdom is the land of the Creator

Only this land is the land of Truth

Where there is eternal life

Stop your wandering

Repent and be reborn as Truth

Then you will know the ways of the world

But man seeks such wisdom

Outside himself and thus cannot achieve it

Look within yourself

# Enlightenment Is Faith

People save people

People save the universe

Heaven and earth are alive within man

Heaven, earth, and humans are alive within man

Let us all go to the land of the true mind

Let us all go to the land where people have the true mind

Let only the land of completion live by becoming Truth

Where all is one

Cleanse your false mind

Cleanse your body and mind

Which are nothing but attachments

Become the forever-living, never-dying Truth itself

Be reborn as the energy and light, Truth


'Coming in a cloud'

'Resurrection from the tomb' and 'salvation by belief'

Let us accurately understand and believe the phrases

Faith is the mind becoming Truth

Faith is when the mind believes

Faith is enlightenment to know Truth

As the mind heads towards Truth

Faith is to become closer to Truth

As much as one has been enlightened


What does 'resurrection from the tomb' mean?

People are dead within their conceptions and behaviors

Accumulating such minds within themselves

That is not the true mind but the false mind and delusion itself

People who are in such delusion are dead

Coming out of the false mind, the delusion

And being reborn as Truth

That is resurrection and infinite life itself

That is to be reborn and resurrected from the tomb


What is the meaning of 'coming in a cloud'?

When there are clouds in the sky

We cannot see the sky because the clouds cover the sky

Likewise, even if Truth were to come among us

People do not know that Truth has come

Thus the meaning of 'coming in a cloud' is

That Truth comes hidden in the clouds

It means the coming of Truth cannot be seen


永生 天國 大情國

The everlasting heaven; the land of great compassion

順理國 人間完成國

The land of nature's logic; the land of human completion

天人地合一國

The land where heaven, man and earth is one

宗教和一 世界合一

Religion becomes one; the world becomes one

創造主國

The land of the creation

復活 在生 全體心化

Resurrection; to live; to become the mind of the whole

眞理自體化

To become Truth itself

一體全體有一

The individual and the whole are one

眞理無門 生時永生天國

Truth has no doors (Truth has no hindrances and is
omnipresent); to become the eternally living heaven while
living

人間主人 本來生國

Man is the master; the land which has always existed

唯一神國

The land of the sole God

新天地國 一體人間心內有

The land of the new universe; everything exists in the mind of
man

# Only People Who Go To Heaven While Living Can Live In Heaven

People whose consciousness is living will live and those whose consciousness is dead will die.

In general it is accepted that we go to heaven or hell after death, but if we do not become Truth now, we already live in hell.

When we watch a movie we become involved in it. We must follow the movie as it is written in the script. The way we live is the same as this in the sense that we live following the script written in our minds as we would if we were watching a movie. Just as the movie is not real, neither is the script in our minds. People live according to this false script of the mind not only while they live in this world but also after they die.

What is on film is not actually visible. However when it is projected, what is on the film becomes visible. Likewise, people's minds, invisible at first, can be seen when projected, for which the way one lives and one's shape are projections of one's individual mind. People's destinies are limited to the script of their minds. The life which they have been living makes their shape now, and the way they are living now will determine their future.

People's minds are the same as their shape. People store in their shape the minds of what they see, hear and feel throughout their life. People have anguish and desires because they are controlled by the countless different minds they have. Thoughts are the human mind which is in fact anguish and desires. In Buddhism, this is called the mind of 'desire, anger, and ignorance' and 'seven feelings and five desires'.

The root of this mind is the life one has lived. We must pull it out, and when that entire mind is discarded, it will disappear. The body and mind are not separate, but one. Even the shapes of the cells in our bodies are the same as our minds. This is because everything that is in our minds is embedded in every single cell of our bodies. This is why even after cleansing the mind we must cleanse our habits that are stored in our cells. One's mind is the life he has lived, which is karma, and the body is where the mind dwells. One's mind is his body itself. The body is one's habits.

Karma and habits are the conceptions and behaviors of the mind and when one discards them, he will see the place of Truth. One's conceptions are the way he sees things. One's behaviors and habits are the embedded desires of what he sees. People only know that which they have come to experience through their lives. If one is asked to speak the language of Uzbekistan, for which he is uneducated in, he will not be able to speak it, nor can anyone speak Malay if they have not learned it. People store their experiences in their minds. Such minds make judgments and people live as slaves to those judgments. They live only for their narrow self-centered minds which consists of what they have seen and felt. When this world is destroyed, when this false world of hell is destroyed, only the world of the Creator exists. This is heaven, the place of Truth.

Generally speaking, people say heaven exists; some best-selling authors go so far as to say they have been to heaven. However, there is such a thing as the heaven of the false mind, the heaven of hell; this is a delusion. Even though one says that he can see heaven through the opening of one's spiritual eyes, it does not necessarily mean that he himself can go to heaven. Such a heaven is not real but is a self-centered delusion.

Real heaven is the land of complete Truth. It can only be seen by those who become complete Truth. True righteousness is to know with wisdom rather than simply seeing heaven. Knowing with wisdom only comes by being reborn as the body and mind of the universe, the Creator of the infinite universe.

One must be free of his individual conceptions and habits, and become the originally-existing Truth in order to go to heaven and the world of Truth. In this world there is no individual and there is no whole. Each individual is the whole and the whole is the individual. This is the world where only Truth, which is one, exists.

When a person has his body he lives by the energy from food, and lives in his delusional mind. When he stops eating and his body dies, he who has a delusional mind will completely die. That delusional mind is false. One's past memories are his mind, and thus, he dies for that mind is false and not true. He will live in the false world, which is not true. The false world is the mind that each individual has and it is embedded even in one's cells. Therefore one's body is not Truth, and he will live forever in the false world which is non-existent like a dream. He will live continuously being reincarnated in the false world forever; he lives in a dream which he can never wake from. This is hell.

In other words, since one is reborn as the soul and spirit of the universe, Truth, he no longer has death and lives forever. Thus, heaven is a place where he who no longer has his individual mind – he who is complete – lives. Heaven is not a place one goes to after death but the place where people are reborn and become Truth while living. Heaven is not a place where somebody, be that a savior, can take a person to after death. Only people, who are reborn from their narrow, limited, individual minds to the infinite, widest, biggest mind of the Creator, can live in heaven. Only Truth can live in heaven. Falseness cannot live in heaven. Those who become true while they are still alive can go to heaven.  Those who have heaven while they are still alive can go there.

# Only Those Who Go To Heaven While Living Can Go To Heaven

Heaven is the land of Truth; it is the Creator of the universe, energy and light, and the Great Soul and Spirit. The land of Truth is God itself, who created the great universe. It is the living God itself that existed before the beginning and exists after the beginning. It cannot be discarded no matter how hard we try. This existence alone is the living existence and only this is Truth. Only this existence is the way, Truth and life.

We must have the widest, biggest, lowest, highest, and cleanest mind without self to become the existence of the universe itself. This is the way to heaven. This existence of the universe is the only Truth there is and becoming it means becoming Truth. One cannot live without being reborn as the body and mind of this existence of the universe. Only this existence is life; only it is energy and light itself. No one can go to heaven without becoming this existence. A person's mind is full of attachments, self-centeredness, his conceptions of the shape of his individual self and even his own world which is hell. When he discards this mind, then the real world as it is becomes his mind, wherein heaven, earth, and humans exist; the world would be heaven and heaven would be in his mind.

No one can live forever without his mind being reborn as the Creator, Truth, while living. No one can live without being Truth while living. Thus, one must be a true person to live forever. If I am not true now, I will die when my body dies. I will die because what is not real is fake.

Some people have the illusion in their false minds that someone will physically take them to heaven. However, going to heaven is when the mind becomes Truth. It does not mean that someone will take us to a place that we think is heaven somewhere in the world.

This universe, made by the will of God, is the most beautiful place. Your mind will become Truth and you will live forever right here in this land by being reborn as the body and mind of Truth.

For those whose mind does not become Truth, they will die completely when their bodies die. They will never be awakened from the illusionary false dreams for their minds are not Truth. This is hell. This is death.

# Real And Fake

This world is Truth as it is, but people make their own illusions and dreams. Because of their illusions they make the fake look real and they also sell the fake as being real.

Real completion of humans is to become the never-changing Truth. It is for his body and mind to be reborn as Truth.

People appear to know a lot of things, but such knowledge is mere self-centered words from their minds of attachments. It is important to know that man does not actually know anything. One's self-centered mind is the mind of what he has learned in this world from his selfish desires.

Real is Truth and fake is falseness. If people do not become real now, they will completely die after death because they are not Truth. People must be real while they are living. They cannot go to the real world if they do not have the real world while they are living; indeed, they cannot go to the real world. All that is fake will die.

To be complete and to live forever is for humans to be

reborn and live as the body and mind of Truth and have the land of Truth.

There have been imitations of clothing, which stirred a lot of noise at one point. People also make artificial food and imitation accessories, but all of these are not real. Although these are all part of man's daily occurrences, man himself must be real. This is because the real will live and the fake will die. This is the difference between true and false, the real and the fake. This is the difference between life and death, existence and non-existence.

The place where everything in this world comes from is invisible to people, yet it does exist. People are unable to become complete while living in this world because they do not know the way to be reborn as Truth, which is within them. People speak and live according to what they have learned. That is all they know. Likewise, if people have Truth in their mind they will know Truth and they will become Truth.

# Everything Is Made By The Mind

When there is no sun

The world is dark

When there is sun

The world is bright

If there is day

There is night

If there is the sun

There is the moon

And the Earth

Because there is this and there is that on Earth

Every creation is born

All is alive

The entire world is alive

Every creation is alive

Therefore the world is perfect

When everything does not exist

Everything exists

And the Creator is

Within humans


Who can save or kill Truth?

One's own mind determines life or death

People with Truth in their mind

Will live

People who have false in their mind

Will die

# People Living In A Dream Do Not Know They Are In A Dream

Dreams are the illusions of people's minds. The mind expresses itself through dreams –what it desires, what it has.

When we are dreaming, we do not know it is a dream. Likewise, people who live in the false world of their own conceptions and standards do not know that that world is a dream. Because they have self-centered false illusions in their minds they know no other way to live but according to their own frame of mind, the script within their minds. It is the same as being unable to avoid the dreams they are dreaming. Only those who have awakened from their dreams know this. Whether you were troubled or in love inside the dream, when you wake from it you know it is not reality. Likewise, life is just a night's dream. When you come out from your own frame of conceptions and standards you will know that life in this world is a dream.

Once you become Truth you will realize that your conceptions and standards are false. You will know that they are just individual narrow thoughts and self-centered principles. Therefore, all of one's own conceptions and standards are false; they are far from Truth.

Truth is life itself. Truth does not have discernment. Truth exists without the mind of existing. It is energy and light; it is great freedom.

One whose current life becomes Truth by awakening from his dream becomes Truth, knows the true world and knows that life is a dream.

# Truth Is As It Is

Birds fly

Animals crawl

Humans walk

Everything lives life according to its shape

Once its body dies here on this earth

It cannot come back with that body

This is the law of the universe

This is Truth

Everything as you see it is Truth, as it is

One whose mind becomes the body and mind of Truth

Lives forever without death in the kingdom of God

The laws of the universe or the laws of nature are

Truth itself

Everything in this world lives in order to live

However nobody knows what living is and what dying is

Because man's consciousness is dead

Everything is dead because humans are ignorant

A dead person knows

Neither wisdom nor ignorance

Nobody knows

When the universe is in man

When man becomes the universe and sees the world

This is wisdom

When your mind and body are reborn

As the mind and body of Truth, God

You will have wisdom

You will know the laws of the universe with that wisdom

When you discard this world and your self which are hell

Only the everlasting universe will remain

When the irremovable, indestructible existence of Truth

Becomes one's mind

When one becomes Truth itself

He will have eternal life and this place here will be heaven

When your mind becomes Truth

You know everything

You know that you are the owner of heaven, earth, and humans

You know that this universe is in you

You know the laws of nature and

Know what life and death are

You see truly, know truly

And live with the world forever in this world without death

You have the whole world in your mind

Therefore you are rich in mind

The world in your mind is your own

And it exists forever as it is

# chapter two

## Why Humans Live And What Humans Live For

# People Can Neither See Nor Hear What They Do Not Have

---

The universe is the wind

The universe is before the wind

Now is the time for everyone to know that

The universe is living

But people who live in their dead world

Do not know this because they are dead

One who knows this feels helpless

He speaks to the dead but the dead can neither hear nor see

Because they do not have Truth within

They cannot understand this

I feel sorry for them

# Eternal Life And Heaven Must Be A Reality One Who Is Not Complete Now, One Who Does Not Have Heaven And Eternal Life Now, Cannot Go To Heaven After He Dies Because He Does Not Have Heaven

The reason humans do not have wisdom is because they do not know anything except what they have experienced and what they have learned throughout their lives. For example, Christians and Buddhists speak only of what they know from what they have learned and heard from their respective religions; and so they would not know about Hinduism.

Each person builds self-centered conceptions for his own convenience and thinks that only his conceptions are right. Often people think that if something fits their conceptions then it is right while if it does not then it is wrong.

This is more apparent when it comes to religion. People accept only what is consistent with their religious beliefs and judge others as being wrong. Some denominations have been labeled as heretical even within the same religion. Even two thousand years ago, when Jesus said, "I am the Son of God," people argued over this. The Jewish people claimed that he was a heretic, a son of a carpenter, not the Son of God because his shape looked the same as theirs. The Bible says people look at the shape but Jehovah sees the inside. There is also a saying that Truth can only be recognized by Truth. Likewise, there is no one who can see and know the consciousness that is within humans. The Jewish people did not recognize the Son of God within Jesus then, nor do they now. Similarly, there is no one who will be able to recognize the coming of the person who has Truth within. The Jewish people are still waiting for a fantasy Messiah of their conceptions because they are bound to the Old Testament, for which their Messiah has yet to ever come.

If today's Christians wait for the coming of Jesus Christ of the New Testament as the Jewish people have waited for the fantasy Messiah of their conceptions, they will not know even if the new world, the days of Truth, has come. They will be no different from the Jewish people.

The ultimate purpose of each religion is to live forever after death, to live forever in heaven after death. However, they cannot go to heaven while they are living because they do not have a practical method of going to heaven. In Christianity they believe that a savior will take them to heaven; Buddhists believe heaven will be fulfilled when the Buddha comes; and old Korean prophecies speak of Jungdoryung; a man of Truth, who will someday come. However, people will be unable to see or hear even though a savior, Buddha, or a man of Truth comes because they are trapped in their conceptual frame of mind.

Only when the person who speaks the method of becoming Truth is Truth, can that person make others become Truth. To be saved is to become Truth; resurrection means to become Truth.

One must become the real Truth while living. Heaven is the real world, and only when it exists can one live in heaven. A person who is not real while living and who does not have the real kingdom cannot go to heaven which is the real world. If you do not become Truth, you will never know this.

You must be in heaven while living. Your body and mind must be reborn as the body and mind of Truth. If not, there will be no heaven where there is eternal life without death.

# Only When The True Existence Comes As A Human Can Mankind Become Truth

## (Light Is Non-material Existence; So Is Truth)

---

Religions are expressions of the story of Truth in words. The mythological story of Dahngoon is about the Korean nation and how it came to be. It is a story about dedication to the welfare of mankind and about people becoming Truth. The Buddhist sutras are about establishing the land of Buddha when the Buddha comes. The Bible is about a savior coming to take people to heaven. Jeungsandoe, Daesoon-Chilihwae, Wonbulgyo (all Korean spiritual practices and religious denominations) also say a great person, a Buddha, will come to accomplish a complete world through enlightenment. In Korea there is a book of prophecy, 'Jungkamnok,' which speaks of the coming of 'Jungdoryung'. No matter what religion, denomination, or faith, all of these are about becoming one, transcending beyond religion, and everyone becoming a completed saint. Furthermore, they speak about going to heaven while living. These existences that have been spoken of are the Creator who created the universe. Completion refers only to the completeness of Truth, and thus, these existences are existences of Truth.

There has been no way for humans to become Truth up until now, for only Truth can teach us the way. Only when there are beans can there be beans. Only cows can reproduce cows, and only Truth can bring Truth.

People speak and live according to what they have within them. Also humans and all creations live according to their shapes. People can neither see nor hear Truth even if it were to come to this world. Humans see and judge the world based on their own conceptions and standards. Moreover, a person's knowledge is limited to what is in his mind through what he has learned from his experiences. These are one's own conceptions. Because there is no Truth within, they cannot see Truth and they do not know Truth. Just as cows reproduce cows and beans bring forth beans, only when the existence of Truth comes as a human can humans become Truth. Only Truth can create Truth. Truth is human completion. People have not been able to become Truth because there has been no true being. If humans could become Truth even if no true being exists, then it is like saying that we can grow potatoes when potatoes do not exist. That is why Christians are correct when they say that completion and heaven can only be achieved by the savior, God. However, we need to look at the Truth inside God, the Savior, or Buddha rather than looking at their shapes. Even now the Jewish people do not believe in Jesus, who said, "I am the Son of God." This is because they believe in a fantasy Messiah of the Old Testament and they do not believe in Jesus as being anything more than a son of a carpenter. As long as people are bound to shape there is no God or Son of God.

People cannot see Truth even if it were to come because they cannot see Truth that is within a person's mind. Each religion has its own conceptions of the existence of Truth for which they wait for its arrival, just as the Jewish people have done. Thus, they will never know or find the existence of Truth if it were to actually arrive. The existence of Truth, the Creator, is the living Great Soul and Spirit itself. Only when that existence comes as a human being will there be eternal life and heaven. People think that the material and non-material are different. However, only when the non-material existence of Truth comes in material form, as a human being, will there be eternal life and heaven while living. Only when people are reborn as that existence will they live.

# People's Conceptions And Behaviors

What are people's conceptions and behaviors? People's conceptions are their false minds accumulated self-centeredly from their past. Behaviors are habits embedded in the body as a result of these conceptions. That is to say, conceptions are the frame of one's self-centered mind and behavior is what that frame of mind has embedded in the body. In order for humans to be reborn, completed, and recreated, one must become Truth and be completed by becoming free of these conceptions and behaviors.

Due to differences in conceptions there is conflict of opinions between husband and wife, between siblings, and between parents and children. In political, social and religious fields there are continuous quarrels caused by each side claiming that they are right. People either think the popular idea is right or that their own conceptions are right, but actually none of these are truly right. What is truly right is only the true mind, not one's individual conceptions. Even though something is true, many times things are thought to be wrong if they go against traditional conceptions or behaviors.

Because the Jewish people who believed in the Old Testament were waiting for the Messiah of their own conceptions, Jesus died on the cross as a heretic. Also, in Korea, Chadon Lee died while trying to spread Buddhism, and Father Taegeon Kim and many other Christians were martyred. All this happened because people could not accept anything outside their own conceptions.

In politics, it has been common practice that the most opinionated person kills the opponents whose opinions do not fit with his own. However people can live as one, without arguments and quarrels, if they become free from their individual conceptions and are reborn as Truth. They can live according to nature's flow.

Historically many have died or suffered because of mankind's false conceptions and this continues even now. People can become one by becoming free of their conceptions, free of their minds. They can become one by being reborn as Truth as they get rid of their selves that have conceptions and opinions. People can become one when they become free from their own conceptions and behaviors, which they mistake as being right. In the conceptions of today's religion, people will not know the coming of Truth even when it comes, because they are waiting for their fantasy Messiah of Truth just as the Jewish people did. One who is waiting for his own conceptual truth will never find that truth because he wants truth to fit his own conceptions.

# The Most Important Thing In The World

The river is blue, the mountain is blue

The entire universe is heaven itself

But there is no one

Who knows the true meaning of this universe

Easterners prefer to live together while

Westerners value a life of individuality

All have lived self-centered lives

Which have once again been the attachments of their desires

Humans do not know why they live or where they go

All live meaningless life

Because of their attachments to the present life

People live thinking they are right

Because of the life they live

Because of their own conceptions and behaviors

However, because they are humans

They do not know that life is meaningless

People do not know the ways of nature

In fact, they do not know the ways of the world

In fact, they do not know the ways of the original heaven

This is because they are not wise

Only when humans are reborn

As the body and mind of the Creator

Will they know everything with wisdom

Only when humans are reborn

As the body and mind of the Creator

Will they live in the kingdom of eternal heaven

As the forever-living, never-dying God

The most important thing in the world is

For one's dead body and mind to be saved

By becoming the living body and mind of Truth

Could there be anything more important than that?

People are burdened with pain while living in this world

Without knowing the reason and meaning of living

Only to die after suffering in their false worlds

The practice of cleansing the mind

Is to become free of one's false mind

To have Truth and live eternally in the kingdom of Truth

Cleansing the mind is repentance, resurrection

And going to heaven

What could possibly be more important than this practice of

Being born again in eternal heaven while living

And living there eternally?

# The Reason And Purpose Of Life

In that land, in that place

There are the earth, those trees

And those houses throughout the seasons

Those trees change with the seasons

Some of the animals stay throughout the seasons

Some of the birds come and go with the seasons

This universe is in the mind of people

 In the icy cold winter

The masses of stars in the sky are frozen stiff

The earth below is frozen stiff

And even the water is frozen

But some birds nevertheless enjoy the cold

Silent nature changes with the seasons

And no matter how many times the seasons may change

The mountains remain and rivers just flow

Nature changes

And the mountains and rivers also change as the years go by

However

The moon, stars and the sun in the sky remain unchanged

Even after

Nature as well as everything in the universe disappear

The sky remains as it was as before

That sky is silent but produces everything in this universe

It is the mother and father of all creation

It is living but is silent

All existing shapes are the embodiment of the sky

People in the world cannot become one

Because no one knows that existing shapes are the sky

Because people do not know this

When seasons pass by again and again

And everything in the universe disappears

With the passing of numerous years

Then this existence which existed forever before, exists now

And will exist forever after

Is the sky, Truth, the universe before the universe

Only a person reborn as the child of the sky

Will never have death

Because he is reborn as the body and mind of the sky

How sad it is for those people in the world

Who have passed away

After living the fleeting years of pain and burden

It is the time for those who are alive now to awaken

And know the true meaning of the world

Do not live like those who have passed away in vain

Blaming the world

Not knowing where to go

Seeking the false world

And not knowing why humans live and what humans live for

Be reborn as the body and mind of the universe

Our precious bodies

Which have been born to live eternally

Must be born again as Truth

And go to eternal heaven while living

Where life and death are one

Truth is the living being

And only when you become it while you are living

Can you go to heaven

If you die without Truth that is death

There would be no eternal life; there would be no heaven

The universe is within one who is living

Therefore he lives forever with the universe

It is my wish that people know this

The reason we come to this universe with this precious body

Is to live forever

Just earning money and eating well

Dressing in finery and living in vain

That is not the purpose of life

I want people to truly know the value of human

The real value of human life

Is to live forever and ever in the everlasting kingdom

# One Lives According To What He Has Within The Mind

The Bible says that God made humans to resemble the shape of God. The shape of God is the place of the Creator, which is the place before all creation. The place before all creation is the place of emptiness where nothing exists. That is to say it is pure emptiness, pure sky. The sole God exists in this place where nothing exists. All creations came forth from this place. Creation is the appearance of this existence, Truth. A state of a person's mind is different depending on whether he is bound to individual shape or has the original mind of the whole.

Humans have the mind of the Creator and so do all creations. God made the mind of humans to resemble the shape of God. Truth, which is God, is the true nature, the original, true mind, and conscience of all creations. There is a saying that people have had sinful minds ever since they 'ate' the fruit of good and evil. This means that they have stored in their minds a distinction between good and evil. Having stored this in the mind is the same as having 'eaten' it. It does not mean that there was actually a fruit of good and evil. As humans began to live in groups they created the concept of sin in their minds. They began to embed the concept of sin in their minds which became their intentions. "Everything happens according to how I make up my mind" is a Korean saying which means that a person lives life depending on what he has in his mind. For example, one who has learned medical science has medical science in his mind. One who has learned law has law in his mind. Therefore, since they have such things in their minds, they will live in the world accordingly. Another example is two people each run hospitals. One hospital runs successfully while the other one fails. This is because the first person has success in his mind while the other has failure.

Even in terms of blessings, a person who is full of the self-centered, selfish, one-sided, false mind, has none while one who has a mind that accepts everything does. One who has a big mind will live with great blessings. Maum Meditation enables people to change their narrow minds into the biggest and be reborn as the wise consciousness of Truth. When people are reborn as the wise consciousness of Truth they will live better lives. The shape of how one lives now is the shape of his mind. These days, people live with self-centered minds, and to live with such a mind is a life of limitations. People who have Truth in their minds will do whatever is true and will put others first. They will save others and will live for others. They will, of their own accord, enable people to become Truth for the sake of all mankind. Whatever they do is for Truth.

People who have become Truth will be reborn and live in the eternal kingdom while they are living, and work for that kingdom. Man's destiny changes depending on what he has in his mind. The most blessed person in the world is one who has Truth in his mind, has been reborn into the eternal heaven while living, and does the work of Truth in the kingdom of heaven. He who lives in that kingdom is one who has received the blessings of heaven; he is one who works for that kingdom and accumulates heavenly blessings.

Mankind has lived with many burdens and pain during the period of incompletion. Shouldn't people know that now is the time when Truth comes to this world and people are becoming liberated from their burden and pain, becoming complete and living eternally? Shouldn't people know that now is the age of living and that they should escape from their false delusions and live as Truth? The reason and purpose for people being born into this world is to live forever like the universe. Because people do not know the reason and purpose of life, they rush about without knowing that there is no place to go. Where are you rushing about, unable to escape from your pain and burden? What are you trying to gain from the meaningless world? Don't you think you should be reborn as Truth, which is life itself, while living, and go to the eternal kingdom of heaven? Don't you think you should live in that kingdom?

People live as a shadow

Holding on to their shadow in their shadows

One who lives the shadows of past memories as himself

Has no Truth

Even though everything is one, Truth

Even though everything is one, trueness

People live as their own shadows

For their shadows become they themselves

When one has Truth, he lives as Truth

Shadows do not exist and are death

Only one who has Truth

Knows the shadow, which is life in the dream

# Truth Can Only Be Known By One Who Has Truth Within

People speak, know, and do only to the extent of what they have within their mind.

People who have falseness in their minds know only what they have learned from the experiences of their lives and they live judging the world according to their own conceptions. People do not know what they have not experienced in their lives nor do they know what they do not have in their minds. Similarly, they do not know Truth as they do not have Truth within. They do not have Truth because they have not been reborn as Truth.

People who have Truth within their mind carry out actions of Truth and work in the kingdom of Truth.

# One World

According to our conceptions, one world refers to a human's lifetime. People grumble that it is difficult to live in this world.

The true meaning of one world is that the whole world is one world. It is the whole world itself; it is not the world of human life, which spans mere 70 or 80 years.

In this one world the living material and non-material existence are one. It is a world where there is no death. It is a world free from birth, aging, disease, and death. One who is in this one world will live forever and this world is the world of God where there is no conception of this and that. That is to say the individual and whole are one and the world of heaven is one world. This one world is the world of the living soul and spirit of the great universe itself. It is the kingdom of the forever-living, never-dying God. It is the complete world of Truth beyond which you cannot go any further. Only one who has been reborn in this one world while living becomes the one world and lives. He lives having been reborn as the forever-living, never-dying energy of God.

# Heaven And Hell

The world where we are living now is the world of hell. The way for humans to leave this world of hell and go to the land of Truth, heaven, is to destroy this hell world of the mind. When you completely eliminate it, the land of Truth exists.

Hell is not the world of God, but the false world of man. Hell is like a dream which does not exist and is false. Therefore, hell is the world where one speaks and acts according to his false mind. Hell is the world where one is bound to his conceptions and behaviors. Hell is the non-existing, false world of death. That world is where one continuously reincarnates and experiences pain within one's delusions.

Heaven is the place where only one who is reborn lives as the everlasting, never-changing, and living Truth, reborn as the original body and mind, soul and spirit. It is the world where only one who accomplishes human completion, Truth, while living, lives. It is the world of great freedom and salvation. It is the world where one who is reborn as the body and mind of God lives forever without death.

# The Definition Of The Sky

---

We often hear that people go to the kingdom of the sky. The question is, 'Where is this kingdom of the sky?' People believe in their own fantasy kingdom of the sky and they believe they can go there after they die.

One who has this sky in his mind will live in the kingdom of the sky and one who does not have this sky, which is Truth, the Creator, in his mind will go to hell. The word, 'heaven' also means the kingdom of the sky where the whole universe is the sky. The true sky originally existed and just existed as it is; however, humans who live with their backs turned to the sky do not know the sky. They do not know the sky because they do not have it in their self-centered, narrow, false mind. When there is no self, not even the universe, then there exists the original sky.

One who goes to the kingdom of the sky is one who becomes the sky by not being bound to the self. One whose mind becomes the sky knows the sky as he has it within his mind. He can see the sky and go to the kingdom of the sky.

The Bible says heaven, the kingdom of the sky, is not something that exists here or there but in one's mind. This means one who is without self and who has cleansed the whole world, so that his mind becomes the sky, is one who is in the kingdom of the sky. He is one who is born in the kingdom of the sky. Only he has heaven in his mind. Doesn't it make sense that one can only be reborn and live in heaven when he has heaven in his mind while living?

Many believe the kingdom of the sky exists in some place and that a savior who will come on a cloud will take them to that kingdom. However, the meaning of 'taking people' is to take people to the kingdom of the sky in the mind. Isn't this more realistic and doesn't this make more sense?

# Only The Savior Can Provide Salvation

Only when a perfect and eternal existence comes to this world, can man become a perfect true existence and live eternally without death in the everlasting kingdom of Truth.

Christians believe that only Jesus, God, can make this happen. They are right. Humans cannot become Truth by themselves. Since the moment this world came to be, there has been no method to become Truth. If someone had become Truth, then his method of becoming Truth should exist. If there were such a method, there should be many righteous people in the world; the world should be one; religions should be one; and the world should be one without separation between nations. The fact that this has yet to happen is proof that no one has accomplished Truth. It is not a question of enlightenment itself but rather the level of enlightenment.

Human completion is to be reborn as both the body and mind of the Creator, Truth. In other words, it is to be reborn as the soul and spirit of the great universe. The human mind can be reborn as both the Great Soul and Spirit of the universe because Maum Meditation presents an eight-level method to reach completion. People who are reborn as Truth are children of Truth and they are complete.

Only Truth can create Truth, only humans can create humans, only cows can create cows, and sweet potatoes must exist in order to create more sweet potatoes. Likewise, only when there is the existence of Truth can people become Truth and live in the kingdom of Truth. This is common sense. Two thousand years ago, when Jesus said he was the son of God, the Jewish people disregarded him, as they thought him to be a mere son of a carpenter, not the son of God. He was accused of being a heretic and was eventually crucified. Two thousand years have passed since Jesus died, yet the Jewish people still do not believe in Jesus all the while believing in the Old Testament.

Like those who continue to wait for the Messiah of the Old Testament, people who believe in the New Testament and wait for their fantasy God, wait for the resurrection of the Jesus of their fantasies, and wait for the savior of their conceptions, will become like the Jewish people.

In the Bible there are the phrases, 'coming in a cloud,'

'coming behind the clouds,' 'coming like a thief' and 'nobody will know.' This probably means that nobody can see the coming of Truth. If Truth comes in a cloud it cannot be seen. If Truth comes like a thief it cannot be seen. Nobody knows because it cannot be seen. Humans live by knowing, speaking and doing only to the extent of what they have within. Likewise, even if a person who is Truth comes to this world people will not know he is Truth because nobody in this world has Truth within them.

In the Bible it says that humans see the shape and Jehovah sees the heart. Likewise, people try to find the existence of Truth in the outer shapes they see. The Jewish people could not recognize Jesus whose consciousness was God, and who was born as the son of God. There is nobody who can see the true existence which is within a person's mind unless he breaks down his own conceptions, his image of the savior. When we look at people passing in the street we do not know what kind of jobs they have and what they think in their minds. In the same way, even if there were a true existence among people, they would be unable to see and know. Truth is not in the shape. People do not know Truth and people cannot even recognize Truth. It is obvious that for one to become Truth and go to eternal heaven while living, only Truth itself can make this possible.

Everything in the Bible and Sutras is correct. However, there are numerous denominations because the conceptions of people who are not Truth have misinterpreted these writings. Those who misinterpreted these writings are most likely the ones who insist that only theirs is right, that others are wrong, and that others are heretics, when in fact they themselves are the ones who may be the heretics. People call others heretics probably because they themselves are the heretics who have a heretical mind within them. What is Truth now is righteous, what becomes Truth now is righteous, and only what goes to eternal heaven now is righteous. Heresy is something that appears to be similar to the real thing but is not. Thus, only the place where one can become Truth now, the place where one can become complete, Truth – only that place is not heretical. The Bible says that one who sells Truth is a prostitute. You must become the real one now. How can you believe that some existence will bring you to the true kingdom after you die if you are not actually living in the true kingdom now? How can you believe that you can go to the true kingdom only after death? You cannot believe this with a hundred-percent certainty.

It is a miracle for a human being to be born into this world with a body, as an existence of one's own. The reason and purpose for a human to be born into this world with a body is to live eternally. Do not gamble this valuable self for vague delusions. The most important thing is to become Truth now and to be reborn in the kingdom of Truth now while living. Do not hold onto your own wrongful conceptions. Discard them and be reborn as Truth.

# True And False

Ask yourself

Whether you are true now

Whether you are a completed person now

One who is not true will know that he is not true

Repent so that you may become true

To repent is to know that sin is not being one with Truth

Because, in your mind

You have numerous, self-centered, attached minds

Whereby you cannot be one with Truth nor be reborn as Truth

If you are the true one now, you will know that you are true

You will live reborn in the true world while living

Heaven is the true kingdom

It is the world

Where only those who have become Truth while living live

It is the eternal and never-dying world

It is not the world where the false live and go to

The false live in the false world

However that false world does not exist and is dead

Only the true live in the true world

The false live in that non-existing world, which is hell

And in this non-existent, false world

Man lives with the burden of pain forever

It is really difficult to come into this world with a human body

Despite cherishing yourself the most

How can you let yourself die, ignorant of the laws of the world?

The most important thing in the world

Is for you to be saved

People come to this world

And live for their selves

And live sustaining their bodies

With energy from the food that they eat

However, the soul and spirit of the universe is within you

When your mind is reborn as that soul and spirit

Where you can live forever and ever, even without your body

Therefore your self can be reborn as Truth and live

Then you are true

A false person does not have the soul and spirit of Truth

Therefore once his body dies it is death itself

A false person lives with the burden of pain

With numerous kinds of stress

A true person has only freedom and salvation

There is no burden of pain and stress in the true world

Even though one lives forever he lives as if it is one day

Only one who has gone to heaven

Will know the state of this true happiness

There is only one lifetime

So please become a true person and live in the true world

The difference between what is true and what is false

Is as different as heaven and earth

The difference between heaven and earth is

As different as living and dying

It is the difference between existing and not-existing

This body lives on energy from food

However one who is born as Truth, the energy of God

Will live as that existence

Regardless of whether the body lives or dies

One who becomes true is rare

One who becomes true is invaluable

One who becomes true is sublime

The most extraordinary person is one who becomes true

# What Is Sin?

Man is a sinner. Man is a sinner because he is not Truth. Man is not Truth because he has created a self-centered self and has false delusions in his mind. This is the sin he has committed during his life time. Humans are originally born into this world as sinners because our ancestors and parents are all sinners. We come to this world resembling the shapes of our parents and that is why we say that 'the apple does not fall far from the tree.' As people have their false mind in their shape which is their body, each of us are the collaborative products of our ancestors' and parents' sins.

People are born with the whole of their ancestors' and parents' sins and karma. Initially, they live as the whole of those sins and then eventually come to have their own minds during their lives; such are original sin and self-created sin. Such sins cannot become one with Truth. People have only self-centered, selfish individual minds that care only about themselves. This is sin. Not to becoming one with Truth is the only sin there is in the world. When you escape from this individual mind and are reborn as the body and mind of Truth, the Creator, this is freedom from sin. Inability to be born again as Truth is because one is not free from sin, which is his own frame of conceptions and behaviors. One can only be totally absolved of his sins when he is reborn as Truth and no longer has his self.

# Nature

The crystal clear river flows silently

Water flows from high to low without fail

The water has fish according to its environment

One must exist for the other

Everything comes forth on its own according to condition

Everything disappears on its own according to condition

Even though millions of things come and go

Everything is the origin of the universe itself

People do not know that

Great nature, which never disappears, is the master

People do not know that

The sky, which is great nature and emptiness, is the master

They do not know this

Because they do not have the sky in their minds

This sky is omnipotence and omniscience, itself

Everything is the embodiment of the sky


Because the sky is living

It brings forth all creations

Thus, it is omnipotent

There is nothing one cannot know

With the wisdom of the sky, God

Thus, it is omniscient

It is not about knowing the tales of human beings

But about knowing

The laws of the origin of great nature, the origin of the universe

Knowing and becoming the sky is the foundation of wisdom

Great nature is life as the embodiment of the sky

# True Love

Love each other

Love means

To accept everything

To accept everything without judgment

Acceptance is

To embrace

Acceptance is

To see as it is, to live as it is and to exist as it is

Discernment of what is what

Derives from the human mind

And exists because of one's own conceptions

That is one's false mind

Everything in the universe is already enlightened

Everything in the universe is already living

Only humans do not know this

Only humans have self

Love is to accept

Love is to have no judgment

One can love only when he is the Creator's mind

One can love only when he is the Great Soul and Spirit of Truth

One can love

Only when his mind is that of Truth and free from his self

True love is only possible for one who has the biggest mind

True love is only possible for the living

Who are reborn as the soul and spirit of Truth

Only Truth can love

True love of the enemy is only possible

When one becomes Truth

Love is to see as it is since you are Truth and without self

True love is

Not to make judgments

Not to have discernment

Great nature gives food and light from the sun

Blows wind and gives water

Without the mind that it has given

That great nature is Truth, love

True love does without the mind of doing

True love is unconditional

A love that is without expectations

True love is the law of nature itself

True love is great

True love does not have a mind of its own

But it is nature's mind, the Creator's mind

It is the mind that accepts everything

The mind which exists but is non-existent

It is the mind that sees things as they are without judgment

# Great Mercy And Great Compassion

Only great nature can have great mercy and compassion

Only great nature brings forth everything in this universe

The mind of great nature never changes

And is the one mind

Therefore it accepts everything


The mind of nature gives us everything we need

Without the mind of having given

It is a mind of consistency and serenity at all times

Even though the mind of the Creator has the entire world

Even though it gives blessings to everything and everybody

The mind of the Creator

Does not have the mind of having done so

But only has great mercy and compassion


True love and true great mercy and compassion are the same

Even though the words are different

They are all the deeds of Truth

# What Is True Compassion?

To truly be compassionate is to be good-natured

To be good-natured is to be generous

To be good-natured is to be tolerant

To be good-natured is to be accepting

To be good-natured is to be forgiving

To be good-natured is to see from another's perspective

To be good-natured

Is to be the mind of great nature, Truth, and the Creator

Only when your mind is Truth, great nature and the Creator

Can you truly be good-natured

This is true compassion

# Nature's Flow

Nature's flow is the mind of great nature

The mind of Truth and the mind of the Creator

The meaning of nature's flow is 'pure logic'

What is pure is nature, Truth

Logic is Truth

Nature's flow refers to Truth itself

As well as becoming Truth

To do according to nature's flow is to do as Truth

Nature's flow is to become Truth

And to live the life of Truth

Love, mercy, and compassion are deeds of Truth

Nature's flow is

To become Truth and to live as Truth

To live according to nature's flow

Means to exist as it is as completion itself

Nature's flow is without conflict, without hindrance

'Purity' and 'logic' mean Truth, the origin

The life Truth leads is the life of nature's flow

Now is the time of nature's flow, when people become Truth

Now is the time when people live according to the flow of nature

Love, mercy and compassion

All mean the life of Truth

Nature's flow is

About becoming Truth and living as Truth

Nature's flow means perfection

Living according to nature's flow means that one is alive

Nature's flow is the life of heaven

Nature's flow is the mind of God

Which never dies and lives eternally

That which is God

Is also nature's flow and the life of nature's flow

Nature's flow is living

It is to become the never-dying God and

To live in the world of the never-dying God

# The Ordinary Is Extraordinary
# The Ordinary Is The Greatest

We think that being the greatest is not realistic. We think that some other great being exists and that greatness exists outside of oneself. True greatness is to just live as is, to exist as is, and to accept everything. True greatness is true nature's mind which has the entire universe. True greatness does not change; it is ordinariness itself. To be extraordinary is to be prominent. However, the person whose mind is the biggest and whose life is ordinary is the most extraordinary and the greatest one.

Greatness is to be the biggest person. We think that the greatest person is one with grand achievements and that to win a war is great. However, to defeat one's self is more difficult than conquering millions of soldiers. The person who defeats his self and becomes Truth is the greatest one.

The person who has become Truth does not have any self. He is the living, everlasting and never-changing God. He lives in the eternal world where only the greatest live.

One who thinks he is the best will die imprisoned in his own excellence and one who thinks he is the greatest lives confined in his greatness. However, one who is just ordinary accepts everything and lives silently and harmoniously with others, and is therefore the greatest and the best. Only one who knows the law of nature and becomes Truth and works for the true world is Truth. This is the one who is the greatest.

# Faith Is Enlightenment Of The Mind

Christians say that if you believe in Jesus you will be absolved of all your sins. Then you will become righteous and a child of God. This is correct. However, there are many who think that merely attending church is faith.

Then, what is the definition of faith? Is faith about diligently going to church? Is praying at each dawn faith? Is singing and preaching well faith? Is reading the Bible often faith? Or is it to pray a lot? The Bible says that those who merely call upon the Lord cannot go to heaven, but that only one who is born again can go to heaven. To be reborn is to be absolved of all your sins. It is to become Truth and to become righteous. It means one has become the child of God and believes in the living God, the Creator, and Jesus.

He who is reborn as the child of Truth, the Creator, is the one who truly believes in Jesus. When your mind becomes one with the Creator, when you are reborn as the child of Truth, it is to be truly reborn. When you have Jesus in your mind that is when you believe in the true Jesus. There is no Truth, no

Jesus, in the human mind. But when one cleanses the human mind and is absolved of all his sins, Jesus is in him; then he truly believes in Jesus, who is Truth. When one has Jesus, he truly believes in Jesus.

One has faith when his mind is enlightened, and enlightenment comes only when he heads towards Truth by absolution of his sins. The extent to which one has Truth is relative to the extent his mind has expanded and has become clear. As this happens one begins to know Truth; and this is enlightenment.

One truly believes only when his mind believes, for which being absolved of all sins is the primary condition. When you are absolved, you will become righteous and be reborn; you will become the child of God. Only a true child of God believes in Jesus. Only those who believe and follow the words of Jesus who is Truth, only those who act according to the words of Jesus, can be absolved of all their sins and become the righteous, the children of God. Only then can people go to eternal heaven. They will be born in heaven while living and work for the kingdom of heaven while living. To be absolved of sin is to accomplish all. To accomplish all is true faith.

# Human Completion Is To Be Absolved Of One's Sins

When I ask people to ask themselves whether they are real, if they are one who has achieved human completion, religious people unanimously answer that they are not. Everybody knows that they are not complete. When I ask people who diligently live religious lives whether or not they can love their enemies or love their neighbors as they do themselves, anyone who is honest says they cannot. Even when I ask whether they can have great mercy and compassion, anyone who is honest says they cannot. Because they have enemies in their minds and because they do not have true love in their minds, they can love neither their enemies nor their neighbors. They cannot have great mercy and compassion as they do not have Truth, which is the mind of great mercy and compassion.

People have become narrow-minded and thus they are far from Truth. There is no Truth in that mind. In that mind are enemies and hatred, self importance, pretentiousness, love, liking, disliking, selfishness, comfort, family, money, and fame. People have accumulated numerous things in their minds while living. Necessary nutrients from food that have been consumed are used in the body, and what is not necessary is excreted. However what the mind takes in cannot be excreted, in the way that the body can. Thus such things in the mind bring forth immeasurable agony and anguish, for which people cannot rest. Because people have false, shadows of the past memories in them, they cannot become one with Truth. This is sin.

Sin is the inability to become the origin, which is Truth. When you cleanse all sins, and are reborn as the everlasting and never-changing Truth, you can reach completion. Only when you are absolved of all your sins can you reach completion.

Just as your body excretes unnecessary food, you can excrete the unnecessary false mind by cleansing the mind, by absolving your sin through repentance.

# The Method To See, Know, And Become The Existence Of Truth

Truth is the existence which has existed before eternity and will exist after eternity. It existed before the beginning and exists after the end, which is after eternity. It is the soul and spirit of the great universe, which is the sky before the sky.

The Bible says God created humans to resemble the shape of God. The shape of God, the original existence, is the soul and spirit, which is the sky before the sky where the one God exists in the place where nothing exists. This existence, which is Truth, cannot be seen and known by people because people only have what they have learned and what they have experienced in their minds. They do not know what they do not have. They do not know God, Truth, because their minds are the size of their own shapes, their narrow and selfish bodies. They do not know God, who is Truth, as they do not have God in their minds.

In order for people to know Truth, they must have Truth in their minds. But people do not know Truth because they do not have it within their minds.

When the minds of people are reborn as wide as, as high as, as low as and as big as the universe, then there is no reason for them to not know Truth, because they have Truth within their minds. The minds of people become one with the existence of Truth when they are absolved of their sins; and herein their minds resemble the shape of God.

When one is reborn as the body and mind of Truth by cleansing his body and mind, his self becomes Truth. He can see and know with his mind since he has Truth within his mind. He will know everything because he is a child of God; and a child of God is Truth.

When people offer up all of their selves to Truth they will live because only Truth will remain. However, one who has his self and tries to put Truth in his self will never obtain Truth no matter how long he tries. Only a person whose body and mind has truly died and has been reborn as the body and mind of Truth, will live forever. A person who has been to Manhattan knows about Manhattan. Likewise, only one who has Truth in his mind can see, know, and become Truth.

# What Are Blessings?

People want to have many blessings. Some lament that they do not have luck with acquaintances; others lament their unluckiness in finances. Some desire good fortune for their children. They ask endlessly for blessings; they want to be wealthy, they want good food and good clothes, they want to have children and hope to meet a good life partner, they want to be healthy, they want to study well and go to a good school and have a good job. Their desires are endless. They ask for blessings through prayer, from fortune teller, or from other beings.

There is a Korean saying that everything turns out according to one's mind. This means that people live only according to what they have in their minds and that their behaviors are determined by what they have in their minds. For example, if they learned medical science in school, they will come out into society and make a living out of the knowledge they have. If they learned law in school, they will work in the field of law. They will work with computers if they learned about computers. Likewise, how we live now is the reflection of our minds. If we have diligence in our minds, we will live prosperously by working very hard, while if we have laziness in our minds, then we will live in poverty for we are lazy.

Let us assume that there are two people who do the same work. While one adapts to the minds of others, the other does not. A person who is able to adapt to others would be more successful in the job than one who is rigid and inflexible to the minds of others. If you do not have good scholastic abilities, you cannot go to a good school. Similarly you cannot get money no matter how much you pray for it. Instead you must work diligently to earn money. It is obvious that results will come about only when one works hard.

Taking action and the way we treat people – all come from the mind. Wisdom also comes from the mind. You will have results the moment you take action. Only when you have blessings will you live well and be happy.

Only when people have blessings in their minds, will they be blessed. But because people do not have blessings in their minds, they do not have it. People's minds are self-centered, so there cannot be any blessings in their minds. In such a mind, no matter how hard one tries, there will be no blessings. Such minds are full of false delusions. When a person cleanses his false, self-centered mind and there is no existence of his self, and when he has the widest, biggest, highest, and lowest mind, which is Truth, everything in the world will turn out well as he is blessed. When there are no conflicts, hindrances, discrimination or judgment, when people accept everything, then blessings will follow. When they have a big enough mind to put everything in, this means that they are the blessing itself and that they have no self; then blessings will follow. Whatever they do would be a blessing itself because there is no self. Then everything will be accomplished.

The greatest blessing in the world is to have the blessing of heaven. The blessings of heaven are to become Truth and to live forever in the kingdom of Truth. When you have the blessings of heaven you cannot help but live well because you manage your life wisely and act with wisdom. You will live with all the blessings of the world. This is the same for all people when they live in this world, for one who is pessimistic with a narrow mind cannot be successful while one who has a big accepting mind, the mind of Truth's blessings, is optimistic. When you are optimistic you can put your ideas into action and when there is action then results will follow. And thus you will have blessings. If you want to be blessed, you must cleanse your mind; you must get out of your passive, narrow conceptions and behaviors and change your mind into the biggest mind. When you do this, everything in the world will be a blessing. You can receive the blessings you wish for when there are true actions.

You will live just as much as you have in your mind, and live no more no less in that frame of mind. But your destiny can completely change when you are reborn; you can accomplish your will. To accomplish, you must have a mind that is big enough to accept it. And your mind will be big enough once you have cleansed it.

# Truth And The Devil – Good And Evil – Coexist In People's Minds

Man's mind was originally the temple of God, the sermon hall of Buddha, and Truth itself. But humans built a citadel of the self in their minds. One's self is his own demon. In fact, man is the greatest demon – the devil itself. And thus it is this devil that lives in the temple of God, the sermon hall of Buddha, holding onto the shadows of false, past memories. Since people live with self-centered selfish minds, they are evil – they are the devil.

Only the existence of Truth is righteous and good. While the original mind is goodness, the minds of people are evil because they have sinned. Since there is both good and evil in the mind, Truth – which is goodness – can drive out the devil.

In Christianity, there is a saying that only God can defeat the devil. This devil is extremely stubborn; therefore only when things fit his conceptions will he accept them, and only when others are nice to him will he accept them. Only the existence of Truth, Buddha, God within him can defeat sin, which is the devil. Only when the devil is broken, defeated and is completely cleared from your mind will you have eternal life and heaven and live in the kingdom.

In the battle between good and evil, only when good is victorious can humans accomplish completion. But if good is defeated, humans will die. Only God, which is goodness, can make mankind accomplish completion and go to eternal heaven.

# Now Is The Time For Humans To Be Created And Live

A long, long time ago

There were no human beings in this world

Through various events

And various conditions

In the midst of different existences

Humans were born

Although the Creator exists just as it is

Humans and everything in this world

Came from the harmony of the universe

By the will of the Creator

For the Creator is perfect

Everything is alive according to the will of the Creator

For the Creator is perfect

Only one who becomes the mind of the Creator

Can know this

Humans being born and living is the will of the Creator

And allowing many to live

Was the unintentional will of the Creator

For an age of formation

Then there is an age of growth and of fruition

During the period of fruition

Humans accomplish completion

Koreans have said

The right path which makes everything one will come

In age of completion

While Christianity says the Savior will come

Buddhism says the Buddha will come

Wonbulgyo, a type of Buddhist religion, says Buddha will come

Jeungsandoe, a type of Tao practice, says a great being will come

They all say the period of completion will come

One should be in the season of fruition

Now is the time, the autumn of Earth

Now is the time for all humans to become complete

By being born in the kingdom of Truth

The new beginning of the universe

Is the rebirth of the consciousness

Rebirth of man's consciousness

Is for the body and mind of man to be reborn as Truth

This is when

This land, this world, exists in the minds of people

Which are Truth, while living

This is when

This land, this world, becomes the land of Buddha, and heaven

Now is the time for all to live

Because they are Truth, they are forever-living

Because they are Truth, they live without life or death

This land, this place, is heaven

And where there is no life and death

One who has reached completion while living

Is completion itself

Even though the flesh dies

One whose body and mind is Truth,

One who has been born unto the kingdom of Truth

Will live without death

In this world, our bodies and every creation

Comes and goes according to condition

But in the kingdom of the perfect Truth, one who becomes

The soul and spirit of Truth, body and mind of Truth

Becomes Truth

And thus he will live forever

This is resurrection

This is the realization of heaven on earth

No one in the world can live

Without being reborn as Truth

Resurrection means the resurrection of the soul and spirit

It is not resurrection of the body, the flesh, after it has departed

the world

Only one who is reborn as the holy soul and holy spirit

Which is the body of Truth and mind of Truth

The soul of Truth and spirit of Truth

Lives in the kingdom of Truth forever

In the kingdom of the holy soul and holy spirit

In the kingdom of the body of Truth and mind of Truth

In the kingdom of the soul and spirit of Truth

He lives because

The holy soul, holy spirit, and holy child are one

The body of Buddha, mind of Buddha and incarnation of

Buddha are one

The body and mind of Truth are one

# The Existence Of Truth

The existence of Truth is the origin of all creation, the principle of Truth. This existence existed before the beginning and exists after the beginning. No one can know this existence of Truth without completely becoming this existence.

What people know is what they have within their minds from learning and from their experiences. Likewise, no one will know Truth if he does not have Truth within. One can know everything in the world by taking it into his mind; yet Truth cannot be known without becoming Truth. I found that those who have their own false conceptions of Truth tend to compare and examine the truth they know to Truth itself during meditation. It is difficult for such people to practice meditation because they have this additional layer of falseness.

Truth is not something one engraves into his head, but instead one has to have Truth in his mind by cleansing it. The existence of Truth is the sky before the sky, which existed before eternity and will exist after eternity. It is the soul and spirit of the universe, which created the universe. It is the Creator, the existence of Truth. One who becomes this existence can see, know, and become Truth. The Creator is Truth; it is the mother and father of all creation.

When one throws away his conceptions and standards, which are in his mind, and throws away his body, then only Truth remains; only then is his mind Truth itself. This is what it is to become Truth and achieve human completion. When one is that existence, then he is Truth. Truth cannot be achieved with your head, but rather you must know it in your mind according to how much you have become Truth; this is enlightenment. Your mind can accept only as much as it has expanded. Only one who has become the complete Truth so as to become the biggest mind can know Truth.

# Great Nature

Birds singing, insects chirping

The sounds of beasts in the dark

Trees and grass are thick

After resting from the heat of the day

There are the beasts that move in the night

This deep, deep forest is no different from ancient times

I try to figure out how many have come to this place

But I do not think anyone has come looking for it

All the while nature stays silently in its place

People think nature has unheard complaints of its own

But nature just stays as it is

With no mind of having done so

The mind of nature is the mind of Truth

In the mind of Truth

There is no mind of individuality at all

It stays as it is without judgment or discernment

Water flows from high to low

Running into trees, stones and moss

So clear that it is almost white

The water tastes sweet

And upon its surface, water drops roll like crystals

The water runs along the valley

To become the river, to become the sea

The sea is a composition of the rivers and the sea

And thus, salty

It changes to vapor to become rain

And rain falls to land

Round and round in circles it goes

On the highest mountains

There are no trees and grass

Because conditions do not allow for them to exist

Likewise, people who regard themselves too highly

Have no one around them

# What Is Pride?

Pride is protection of one's self

Which is a false existence

True pride is to have Truth

One's mind consists of the accumulation of false images

One lives with that mind

And so the narrower his mind, the stronger his pride

When there is no mind of one's self

He lives as it is, even when he faces confrontations

He lives as it is, even when he must face the wind

He lives like the wind, like water

He lives just as he is, just as he is shaped

Everything is one; everything is Truth itself

However, in the narrow, selfish minds of humans

There is no Truth

One cannot live like wind and water

Because his mind cannot become the wind and water

Because it cannot become great nature

When one is rid of all conditions

And throws away all of his desires

He sees all as it is and lives as it is

He is the highest one

Even though he may suffer loss in the world

He lives silently

For he is the highest one

Only one whose mind becomes the mind of nature

Has no enemies

A person with the mind of nature hates no one

When there are no images of the shadows of one's memories

And only Truth remains in his mind

Then he is one who has been reborn as the mind of nature

Because he is great nature itself

He is one who is one with nature

# Story Of Life

Wind blows roughly

Flashbacks of past memories hit me like tidal waves

They are meaningless memories

Yet they have become yearnings

I am currently in my midlife

And as I look back to those numerous days of

Happiness, agony, and loneliness

I feel I have accomplished nothing in my life

Like I have done nothing but lived for my body

While the years passed by

I lived without knowing reason and purpose

What is a life of righteousness?

Why do people live?

Why should people die?

What is life?

Everyone lives in a meaningless dream

And just disappears without reason or purpose

All of my bitterness due to my discontent

Was just a dream of my greed and desire

I was not the only one

Who lived lonely days and a lonely life

But I had such loneliness

Because my mind existed

Never was I able to truly laugh

And never had I experienced true delight in my past

I had no beautiful memories

For which this absence became a bitter discontent

Many people envy me as I am the ultimate Truth

What people envy me for is

The recognition and acknowledgment that I receive

People do not treat me with sincerity

But with their minds of greed and desire

Which are the shadows of falseness

I do not like this

So I leave them after I have taught them

When they begin to recognize who I am

I leave for I do not like people

I want people to cleanse the dirty mind

To cleanse the sin of attachment

And become clean like me and to know all the ways of nature

As it is written in the 'Kyeogamourok'

An ancient Korean book of prophecy,

'Man seeks the heaven to come with a snake-like mind'

In order to fulfill their own desires

People do not repent their sins but expect me to do everything

And they only look at my appearance

They have only a mind of trying to gain

I teach them that

Anyone who is absolved of all their sins

And who becomes Truth because he is clean

Will live forever and ever in the kingdom of heaven with me

Although the wind blows and rain falls

Although blizzards rage and there are dark clouds

Although there may be heavy fog

Although humans may change and everything may change

The true world does not

And thus I wonder, when will it be

When people come to the world that is good to live in?

When will the day come

When human's attachments are no more?

People live according to their desires

They do not go to heaven where they should truly live

They are just aimlessly busy

Without knowing reason or purpose

They are endlessly busy

Because they live according to their own false minds

Because they live as their false minds tell them to

And thus there is no meaning and no reason

However

There is nothing that remains and nothing that can be kept

People live without purpose, not knowing where to go

They live deceived inside their false minds

They live trapped in their delusional minds

I wish and wish again that everybody would come to

The kingdom of Buddha and God

By tirelessly repenting their sins

But people who need to absolve their sins the most

Are dead and trapped

And thus they do not know

How frustrating their lot is since they are dead

Only the living can become a doctor

Who can make the dead live

And only he is frustrated

Not just a few, but many people are dead

In fact, six billion people are dead

That is why the doctor of the soul and spirit

Who can make the souls and spirits live is frustrated and busy

I was busy in my life before and now only I am busy

Working as the doctor of the soul and spirit

But it is indeed worthwhile

To make people's souls and spirits Truth

And to let them live in the kingdom of the soul and spirit

This is all I am devoted to; this is the only thing I do

I help people to cleanse their past shadows

I ask them to become Truth and live

And tell them that human completion is the only way to live

I ask them to go to the perfect kingdom

The bright kingdom of light

The living kingdom, the kingdom of hope

The kingdom of life, the true kingdom

The forever-living kingdom of resurrection

The ideal kingdom humans dream of

# An Enlightened Saint Is A Completed Person Who Has Been Reborn As The Existence Of Truth

Enlightenment is the original place of everything in the world; it is the Creator and Truth. To be enlightened means to be reborn as this, as the original place, the Creator and Truth. To become a saint means the same thing.

When the existence of Truth becomes one's mind, in other words, when I am reborn as the body and mind of Truth – the original body and mind – then life and death are one; it is eternal life, heaven on earth and the Land of Buddha. When people become this existence and are born again in the kingdom of heaven on earth as a saint while living, then they are Truth. They will live eternally in this kingdom. People think that both being reborn and resurrection mean for the body to be resurrected, when actually it is the resurrection of the spirit and soul, which is the mind. Heaven is the land of that living soul and spirit and the land of Truth. People who become complete will live eternally in this land of the soul and spirit where everything is alive. Only people who are reborn into this world are saints; they are complete people.

# The Most Important Thing In The World Is To Come Out Of One's Tomb And Live In The Land Of Light

Do you know why you live?

Or what it is to live a true life?

Do you know why you were born?

Or what the true purpose of human creation is?

Do you know what you live for?

Or what the true purpose of life is?

Without an answer, without a purpose in life

People live only for their bodies, for good food and good clothes

All they know is a life in which the body is everything

Where they live only for themselves

Not knowing that they are trapped in the tomb they have dug

They do not know about the world outside of the tomb

The land of light

Land of freedom

Land of Truth

The living land

They do not know the land outside where there is no death

They cannot see, hear or have that land

This itself – the inability to see, hear or have that land – is death

How can a dead person know whether he is alive or dead?

Only a living person knows what is dead

And only a living person knows what is alive

The most urgent thing in the world is

To come out of one's tomb

Instead of being trapped living in it

This world is a tomb

People who are trapped in this tomb

Do not know they are in it

This world is the world of hell

But people do not know they are in hell

Likewise, how can people know the world of Truth

When they do not know Truth?

People only have what they have experienced

Thinking that that is knowledge

They only know as much as they have learned

People do not know the true land of Truth

Because they do not have it in their minds

In the hell world

They are busy doing useless, unnecessary things;

They think that is all there is

Though they may busily scurry about

There is no place to go

What is the use of gaining something

Within the delusional, false world?

What is it that you have actually gained?

In their delusional false worlds

People hold on to what is actually fake

Thinking that it is theirs, thinking they have it

Thus their lives are without purpose or meaning

What is the purpose of man who were born

With only one life as a human being

If this world is the end?

What is the purpose of humans?

The most urgent thing is

To come out of one's tomb, the false world

And to live forever without anxiety or worry

In the land of eternal Truth

The land of bright light

The living land

Why is it that you are unable to go

To the place you must truly go to

Even though you have no place to go

Even though you have nothing to be busy about?

One should live while living

One should go to the living kingdom while living

The ultimate purpose of human life is to live

He who does the work of the living kingdom

Is an enlightened person

Who knows all

Who has accomplished all

One must accumulate his own blessings in that world

He will live forever with those blessings

Because they are his

Such a person is the most extraordinary

And the wisest in the world

But the dead continue to build their tombs in the dead land

# Tales Of Going To Heaven

There is a saying in Korea that one can forget all of his past if he drinks from the 'spring of life' after he dies. What this actually means is that when the mind and body of one's self dies and the universe disappears, then they will no longer exist, and the world of Truth – the origin of life, the world of the great soul and spirit, life itself – will appear. One can forget all of his past as he is reborn as Truth, because the conceptions and behaviors of his past hell world no longer exist.

This world is the material world, but the kingdom of Truth, which has received the life of the soul and spirit, is the true world that is forever-living and never-dying. You will know this when you cleanse all of your self while living, which is to thus drink from the spring of life. Also, there is a saying that you will know the afterlife only when you die. Indeed, you will know the afterlife when you completely die while living. This is like saying you will know Manhattan only when you have been to Manhattan; you will know only what you have experienced.

There is an old tale about a man, long ago, who went to a wise man to learn of Truth. The wise man said to him, "Go work ten years as a servant." After working ten years the man returned to the wise man, for which the wise man told him, "Go jump off that high tree next to the pond." It is said that when he jumped he went to heaven. What this story actually means is that because he jumped in his mind and died in his mind, he was able to go to the true land, the kingdom of heaven.

There is also another tale, an old Korean story about a girl named, 'Shimcheong' which means 'clear mind.' In this story, the blind man, Shim, sacrificed his only daughter Shimcheong to Buddha, the existence of Truth, and soon after he could see. The story is about being born in the new world, the kingdom of Truth, for when Shimcheong is sacrificed, she falls into sea and dies, but then is resurrected in the underwater kingdom of the Dragon King where she becomes his queen. Here, the kingdom of the Dragon King is the kingdom of Truth; to drown in the deep sea means the death of the existence of one's self.

In the story, Shimcheong becomes Truth and returns to the human world with the true mind. This story is about how the blind Shim actually had a mind that was blind, and that the eyes of his true mind opened when he met his daughter, Shimcheong who was Truth. This means Shimcheong and her father opened the eyes of their minds by completely giving up their selves as well as what was theirs.

Another story is about a woodcutter and his wife who was a nymph. A deer wanted to return a favor to the woodcutter who had saved the deer from a certain death. The deer told him a secret method for keeping his wife from running away. The deer told the woodcutter that he must take the nymph's wings away from her and not return them until she has had three babies. But, as time passed, he began to pity his wife, and gave the nymph her wings when she had had only two babies. This meant that she could carry a baby in each arm and fly back to heaven. A while later, after his wife left him, the woodcutter was also able to go to heaven. However, as time passed, he wanted to see his mother, who he had left behind on Earth. He begged his wife to help him return and visit his mother. And so the nymph gave him a horse to return to the Earth on, but warned him never to dismount from the horse because once he sets foot on Earth he would not be able to ever return to heaven. With his wife's warning in mind, the woodcutter came down to Earth and visited his mother. Later, as the woodcutter was about to leave, his mother asked him to at least have some porridge before he went. He did not refuse, and tried to eat it sitting on the horse. But some of the hot porridge fell on the horse's foot. This gave the horse a fright and it bolted forward, throwing the woodcutter off its back and galloping away to heaven without him.

This is a story about how a person should not look back once he has gone to heaven, about how the woodcutter could not go to heaven due to his lingering attachments to Earth, and how he was thus left behind.

# The Most Urgent Thing In The World

People are so busy trying to live, even though they live just like everyone else. They have to feed their families, send their kids to school, and keep up appearances. In other words, they live trying to give their bodies good food and good clothes. The ultimate purpose of learning in school is also to eat well and live well. But no one knows the true values of life, the purpose of those values, and the meaning of life. Therefore, there are no institutions that teach these things.

The reason and purpose of humans coming into this world is to live. 'To live' does not mean to live in this world, but it means to live forever.

One receives his body from his parents who came from the ancestors of both the mother's side and father's side for over numerous years. One was born into this world through the fate which connected my parents at the exact time and day, and without it I would not exist. One's birth is a dramatic event, which could not have taken place had it not been for the specific circumstances of his ancestors' lives.

Thus, each human being is a precious and rare existence. And the reason and purpose of such an existence to come to this world is to live forever. In order to live in this world, to live for their bodies, people live with their self-centered, multi-layered pretentious minds. People store numerous things in their minds throughout their lives, so thus they are dead and buried in their tombs.

Scientists in Scotland were able to clone a sheep using a single cell, which proved that a single cell is the same as me as the whole. Each cell in a person is a miniature version of that person. Even one's cells are dead when his consciousness is dead. The world where people live in now is not the true world, because the world they live in is the world they have in their minds. How one sees the world is different depending on their minds, depending the extent of what they have in their minds. That mind allows them to move and know how to live. But the lives of humans are not true since they live accumulating what they have learned and experienced, which are the shadows of their memories. Such lives are non-existent illusions once people die. But those who have Truth within will not die even when their bodies die.

One's mind is his self, and he who has much falseness in his mind lives a false delusional life in his tomb for he must live according to what his false delusional self orders. Within their tombs, such people believe in religions or practice other forms of meditation to get rid of the burden of pain or to have comfort in their minds. Nevertheless, they are trapped and cannot get out from those tombs which they themselves have created.

For those who come out from their tombs, there is the world, while those who remain dead in their tombs cannot come out. Many have spoken about the world beyond the grave. Some say a savior will come to take us out of our tombs while others say they can get out of the tomb if they have faith. But can anyone guarantee that any of these methods will really work? Only a person outside the tomb can know the method to come out from it.

In the tomb, there are many disguises and fraud; and in the tomb, they speak only illusionary false words which are mere words with no actions. Outside of the tomb, all is free without constraints and everything is as you see it and as it is. People who are trapped in their tombs do not know the world outside as they are dead in their tomb, thinking that the tomb is the whole world.

One who lives in the world outside of the tomb pities the people trapped inside. He also knows they are truly to be pitied because if they just come out from the tomb they could live in the true world. Indeed, it is such a pity for if they would just come out from their tombs they could live in the true world.

People who are trapped in their tombs must come out from them and into this new world and be the owner of the new world, this world. This is the most urgent thing that people should do. This is the only way to accomplish the reason and purpose of why humans are born into this world. One who is reborn outside of the tomb lives life outside and does not return to the life he lived inside it.

# Let Us Live As The Wind

I sang alone

Disliking the world

For the disagreeable world and my mind of grudges

Flew away with my song

I drank

Because I found the world did not fit my will

With every glass that was emptied

My agony would go away

In the frozen winter days

I walked only with the moon as my friend

I walked the fields devoid of people

For I did not know the true meaning of humans' life

And because the world did not fit my will

I just walked aimlessly

I learned about life

And how it vanishes like the vapors

Of what I am unsure is my breath or cigarette smoke

Without reason or meaning

There were many thoughts in my mind

One thought after another

And in my loneliness

There was never a single day when I could laugh heartily

My life was like an endless dessert

A life without answers

But once I disappeared and became the universe

I came to know the principles of the world

Once I disappeared and became the universe

My song

My drinking

My agony

All become free and calm

Because the world sings, the world drinks

And my endless agony is no more

I am always at rest

For only the world exists within me

My songs become

Songs of rest and freedom

I no longer have any songs of regrets

Or questions and doubts

I live as it is, exist as it is

When I disappear and become the world

I exist yet I do not exist, I do not exist yet I exist

The world which is true life, is me

Let us understand the meaning of great nature

And live the life of great nature

Let us know the meaning of all creation in the universe

And know the true reason why the creator made the universe

What man lives for

And why he is born in this world

Is to be the world and to live as the world

It is to live in the world

As one with the world

It is regretful to see

People live as slaves to their own mind

I tell them to

Be the world and live as the world

Do not live as slaves to agony and useless thoughts

Take rest

And be free

In the true world within yourself

Where there is no death and one lives as it is

I tell them to live as the world

Because everything is living and

Existence and non-existence are one

To live as a completed person

Is to become the world


There is no going or coming

There is no coming or going

Everything exists on its own

Everyone who becomes the world lives that way

Everyone who becomes the world

Is the forever-living, never-dying God

Everyone lives with the world as one

The kingdom

Where only those who have the world in their minds live

Is the forever-living heaven

# One Must Know Truth After Becoming Truth
# Do Not Try To Know Truth Through Your Own Conceptions

Humans know Truth only as much as their minds are cleansed because that is how much Truth can fill their minds. A person's body and mind are his own conceptions and behaviors. Many people try to judge Truth using their own conceptions and behaviors without discarding their body and mind. They try to know Truth with their own narrow minds, but they cannot; it is a hurdle that they are unable to get over. People do not know Truth properly because they do not have it within their minds. Instead, they try to know Truth by creating it with their false minds. Just as a silkworm can transform only after it eats enough, people can only have Truth within after they throw away enough of their conceptions and behaviors. To have Truth within means to be enlightened.

Truth is not something that can be understood or known with your head. Truth can only be achieved as much as you become Truth and as much as you have Truth within. Everyone needs time on their path to become Truth. People tend to want to have results without effort; they are impatient, and thus they cannot accomplish Truth. You must cleanse as much as you should in order for Truth to be revealed and in order to become Truth. There is nothing more important than becoming Truth for the sake of Truth. Therefore you cannot achieve Truth with a cunning, snake-like mind.

Even when living in this world, only those whose minds are whole-hearted, strong, and righteous can live well and be successful. They cannot achieve this if their minds are cunning and two-faced, or if they have very opinionated minds. It is the same when you try to become Truth – if your self still exists, you cannot become Truth; if there is no self and there exists only Truth, you will be reborn as Truth. Truth exists only in those who are reborn as Truth. This means that Truth remains only when your self – your conceptions and behaviors – do not exist. For your self to no longer exist, this means that you are reborn as the body and mind of Truth. This is complete accomplishment of Truth and completion. Unless you become this itself you will not and cannot know this.

# Light And Darkness I

The world of darkness

The world of light

Darkness

Is the absence of light

The world of darkness

Is full of false words because one cannot see clearly

False words are lies

And even though many are spoken

People do not know whether those words are true or false

The world of darkness is a dead world

Wherein people live without knowing it is dead

In the world of light

Everything lives because of the light

People can see each other clearly in the light

People can clearly see and know the false world of darkness

Light is the living world

The world of darkness is the world of the dead

People speak of illusionary things

Which they have never seen

Because they see narrowly

They speak of meaningless things

But though there are numerous false words

When the bright day of light comes

Everything will be discovered to be false

In the darkness, the darkness is thought to be Truth

Because people have never seen light

Or lived in the world of light

To live well and accomplish all

Is to live in the world of light where there is life

The mute live even though they cannot speak

The deaf live even though they cannot hear

Similarly, people seem to live in this world,

Even though they do not have light in their mind

People seem to be alive

Because they live by the energy from food

However, in the true world

Only the energy and light of Truth is life

Only a person who is reborn with that life

Will live because he has life

The mind will live or die

Depending on

Whether or not he has illusions in his mind

And whether or not he has Truth in his mind

# The Reason And Purpose Of Human Life

Science tells us that originally hot gases of the original universe exploded and fiery cluster of matter formed; some cooled into stars and others into planets. One religion says that the universe was created by the word of God, and another says that the universe came forth on its own. These theories all seem to be different, but they are actually the same.

The word of God is 'logos,' reason, and original nature. It is the sky before the sky, Truth, the Creator of the universe, and the soul and spirit from which every creation in the universe came forth. Humans cannot see it with their eyes, and because of this, there are those who are atheists.

Not long ago, there was a tsunami that hit Southeast Asia and took the lives of many. But even though humans disappear, the universe remains as it is. Imagine this earth disappears; the sky, which is the universe, will remain as it is. Even though all celestial bodies disappear; the sky will still exist. When human minds become the sky, man will be able to see the Creator and know with wisdom that everything in the universe is created by the Creator. When one's mind is cleansed and he is reborn as the mind of the Creator, he will know the Creator because he will know as much as he has in his mind.

For sure, the Creator – the soul and spirit of Truth – created everything in the universe. Therefore, everything in the universe is inevitably a child of the Creator because the Creator made it. However, when humans have difficulties they question the purpose of their pain and burden saying, "If the omnipotent, omniscient Creator exists and humans were created as complete, then shouldn't the Creator have created humans without pain and burden?"

During the age of growth in the universe, the human population increased because of mankind's greed, so wouldn't it be wise to harvest when the human population has reached its peak on this Earth? Though the Creator has no will, this is the will of the Creator.

The kingdom of the Creator has always been complete, and in it all are living. But only humans cannot become one with Truth because of their sins. This is because they have a self-centered selfish mind, which exists for their body's comfort and splendor. This is sin and karma. Because they have possessiveness in their minds and are bound to themselves, they are unable to become one with Truth, the original master. Their minds are trapped in their tombs, which is death. You will meet Truth when your body and mind – your self – is cleansed. You must be born again as that which is beyond your own existence, as Truth, in order to be a child of Truth. You will live in the eternal, never-dying, living kingdom of Truth.

Truth is the living, never-dying existence. When you are completed, when you are Truth in this universe, you will live forever because you have become Truth while living. You will live forever only when you go to the kingdom of Truth while you are alive. Now is the time when people become Truth – the age of fruition. There is nothing higher than Truth; there is nothing more perfect than Truth; there is nothing beyond Truth. Even though different religions have different terminology for Truth, what religion seeks is this existence, perfect Truth. To become Truth is to become a complete person; it is the only way to live forever.

The reason and purpose why humans live is to become Truth and live in the kingdom of Truth forever. One who does not become Truth during this age of fruition will die.

# The Will Of The Creator

There are different kinds and different shapes

Of beasts that fly in the sky

Depending on where they live

There are different kinds and different shapes

Of beasts that crawl on the land

Depending on where they live

The same goes for the creatures of the water


This is because all come from various conditions

And live in various conditions


Everything comes from those conditions

And lives in those conditions

They disappear when the lifespan of their shapes ends

This is nature's flow; this is Truth


You can know this when you become great nature

Which is the mother of the universe

Only great nature can know the flow of the nature

Because it created the universe

Great nature is all there is in this world

And only when you become the whole, the universe

Will you know the laws of the world


What is the reason and purpose

For all creation to be born and live?

You will never know the answer within your false mind

The reason and purpose for the Creator, great nature

To create the whole of creation

Is to make them be born again as Truth and live eternally

The Creator has no purpose, but this is purpose of the Creator


The Creator does not have a purpose

But the Creator's purpose is to make everything perfect

And let everything live


When humans and the whole of creation

Are reborn as the origin, great nature

This universe will live forever and ever within humans

Those whose minds become great nature are

Great nature itself

In this land there is no death

Because the individual and the whole are one


This land is the living kingdom

This land is the forever-living, never-dying kingdom

This kingdom is only for those who are Truth

And those whose minds are born as the origin, Truth


If there were no humans

This universe would not have any meaning or purpose

It is man who knows that the universe exists

And that the world exists


When humans return to the origin, Truth

When humans are reborn as the body and mind of Truth

They have no death

And they are the masters of the universe

# Vanity Of Life

In order to get to the neighboring village beyond the hills

There is the winter snow frozen on the grass

A big pine tree planted on the burial grounds

And the freezing wind which makes the pine boughs moan

Pierce into my very bones

I travel far, but I have yet to reach the village

Here the owls cry and the wolves howl at night

For countless years

Many people have lived here

Without leaving these mountains and rivers

The evidence of their life, their relics

Are the people of today

There were many stories and events

Of those people who lived many years ago

The present life is the same

Now that I know Truth, I realize that

Those people lived in a dream

And died, bound to their meaningless lives

They insisted on their possessions

However, nothing is left

Nothing is theirs

Only nature does not seek gratification

Only great nature remains silently

Only great nature remains living

Only people live noisily in agony and stubbornness

But they all passed away without a trace

They were unable to just live and die

Everybody died and disappeared in their falseness

The place that the enlightened one sees

Is the place without any traces

People who feel the futility of humans and their lives

Will know that there is no way to live

Unless they become great nature

Only when you return to great nature

Only when you are reborn

As the body and mind of great nature

Will you live eternally like nature

# Trueness And Falseness

One who has falseness in his mind

Passes away after having lived a false life

One who has Truth

Will live a true life

He does not have death, for he is Truth

Everything is living

But humans regard themselves too highly

Because of their own desires

Thus humans are dead, trapped within themselves

The whole of creation lives according to the flow of nature

But instead humans live by their own minds

Their false minds become their selves

And humans live in their false worlds

Doing what their false minds order them to do

A person who has the Creator, the immortal Creator, within

Will have no death because his mind is Truth

Truth exists; what is false does not

Truth is life; falseness is death

# God Is Everything

While the sounds of birds and the sounds of the wind

Are all sounds of God

People look again and again for God

That which exists is God

Everything that exists is God

Humans cannot find God inside his falseness

Because God does not exist there

Therefore, he cannot become God

God is never-dying and forever-living

God is the mind which has the whole of the universe

One who becomes God knows

That the sound of birds and the sound of the wind are God

But one who does not become God

Hears the sounds of birds

As the sounds of birds

And the sounds of the wind

As the sounds of the wind

God and everything are one

The instincts of every creation is God

Living on its own according to its own shape

That itself is the shape of God

Everything, which is existence itself, is born

Because there is existence

The existence that humans do not know is God

For humans do not have existence in their minds

The emptiness of the sky is God

But humans do not know God, the emptiness

As they do not have the emptiness in their minds


Everything is the representation of God

Everything is the life of God

Humans say that this is this and that is that

Which are their own conceptions and behaviors

Each person has a mind of his own

And in that mind he has his opinions

To which he binds himself

However, God is freedom and emancipation

God is the self-existing mind

Which exists but does not exist

It is an empty mind because it knows everything

It has no judgment because it knows everything

It has no thinking because it knows everything

God is always living

Only one who becomes the living God

Knows God

To be enlightened about all, to accomplish all, to know all

Is to be reborn as the perfect God


The life of everything in this universe

Is of one mind which is the life of God

However, only humans are unable to be the great one mind

For they live with a self-centered mind

Everything is perfect in and of itself

Everything lives in harmony, which is nature's flow

Only humans live in the illusion of his world

# Become Nature And Stay

Will you go

Or will you stay?

There is nothing to have in this universe

There is nothing to take from this universe

Will you go

Or will you stay?

If you stay, everything exists as it is

Is it not better to just stay

Rather than depart without a place to go?

Just become nature and stay

# The True Meaning Of Being Extraordinary

To be ordinary means to be the same as the majority. To be ordinary means to be the same as the majority in shape and behavior. To be extraordinary means to be superior and different from the masses.

But to be truly extraordinary in the world is to be ordinary and behave like others do, yet live as the mind of Truth. In the eyes of people, an extraordinary person looks the same as themselves, but they are unaware that his mind is heaven. He lives with the mind of heaven and with that mind he meets others. Thus, he lives as it is, with no hindrances in his mind. He is the most extraordinary person in the world. Generally, people think being extraordinary means being different in speech, actions, behavior, cleverness, power, and uniqueness. However, the most extraordinary person is the most ordinary.

# The Most Important Thing In The World

I drink, then look up at the sky

There is no way to express my mind

I sigh into the empty sky

As I gulp down a bowl of *makkolli* (crude rice wine)

There is no one who understands me

There is no one who can help me

As the years went by my worries were forgotten

And I just steamed ahead like a train

My past became my memories

Memories of the many stories I do not want to think about

Every person has a lonely path to go

But why did I live so busily? Why did the train keep going?

As the years passed I have become mature

And I have realized that that is life

I had lived thinking that I was the loneliest and that

Only I was heavily burdened with pain

I thought only I was burdened

Because I could not see the pain of others

My youth has passed with time

I know that the place I have aimlessly come to

Is the origin of the universe in this period of the universe

I realize now

Why there were so many burdens of pain in my life

Because I existed

I thought that I had to do everything and have everything

All of those minds were useless, futile dreams

Now I understand the stories of saints

And how they must have felt

Now I know that all those saints came to this world

By the will of the living God

The owner of the universe is 'me'

It is 'me' that makes the universe and humans live

By the universe and humans becoming one

The foolish are trapped, dead, within their own minds

People think they are too good

To follow the will of the universe

I teach people the stories of the divinity

The stories of Buddha

And the existence and identity of God

Which has only been spoken of

I let them be reborn as the children of that existence

The reason why

The most mediocre and loneliest person in the world

Such as myself

Had such a life

Was to become Truth

The whole of humanity is dead

Within their own conceptions and behaviors

With painful burdens

But they do not know they are dead

For the dead do not know they are dead

The way to live is to cleanse the self

Cleanse the universe

Return to the origin of all creation

And be reborn as the eternal, never-dying God

Only Truth can do this

People all live a life of their own

The reason they live with painful burdens

Is because they have their selves

When I look in the mirror

The 'me' in the mirror has no worries

A person who becomes God

Is like the 'me' who exists in the mirror

When the 'me' in the mirror exists on its own

Like the 'me' who is outside the mirror

That is human completion

The 'me' outside the mirror

Has countless worries and agony

While the 'me' inside the mirror

Is devoid of the burdens of the world

We come to this world only once

We must all be reborn

As the forever-living, never-dying God

By becoming this one world, which is the whole of the universe

The true purpose of human beings, the true purpose of life, is

To be born again as a complete person, as Truth

This world cannot only have superior people in it

When you listen to what the ordinary person says

And try to do what he suggests

It may well be the most important thing in the world

It may well be the most precious thing in the world

# Education Begins With The Recovery Of Mankind's Original Nature

Since long time ago, scholars have attempted to study the original nature. Some have said that the 'chi,' or energy, of the universe is one, while others have said it is two. When they say that chi is one, they are talking about the existence of the one universe. When they say it is two, they are talking about yin and yang, the body and mind of the universe, which are separate yet one at the same time. Although their words may sound different, they speak of the same thing – that this existence is the original nature and that this existence is the origin of the universe.

Christianity says that to know God is the basis of wisdom. The original nature is what Christians call God. Originally, there is one God, the sole God. And though there are both the Holy Father and Holy Ghost, they are all one. In Buddhism, there is 'Dharmakaya,' the Mind of Buddha, and 'Sambhogakaya,' the Body of Buddha, and though they are two, they are also one. All such things refer to the place of the Creator, to Truth, to the origin and to the master of all creation.

Returning to this existence is the basis of knowledge and wisdom. Because there is wisdom, it is thus wisdom itself and the basis of knowledge. The education of mankind is to return to this existence.

It is generally understood that a well-rounded, complete education includes the learning of knowledge, virtue, physical ability and the arts. However the true meaning of being complete is to be a perfect person, which means to live forever. The existence that never dies is Truth, nature, and the master of all creation; and to become this existence is to become a complete person, a perfect being. This means that one must get rid of his knowledge, conceptions and behavior, and be reborn as the body and mind of the original perfect existence.

Today's education is designed only for living a better worldly life. But when humans come to know the origin and live as the original mind, then all of mankind will become one. We will know how to be thankful to our country, to the world; we will no longer have whimsical minds but trust each other, have confidence in each other all the time and have better lives. But in order to do this, everyone must recover their original mind; then their minds will be one for which there will be no thieves or crime, and everyone will live for each other. In other words, an education that allows us to do the above is truly a well-rounded education for human completion. When there is no concept of 'your country' and 'my country,' all become one and this is our kingdom. But when humans live only for one's own riches, fame, and power, there is nothing to have, or gain; nothing remains. When everybody recovers their humanity, which is their original nature, they will live diligently because everyone's minds are one and thus, are not whimsical or sly. Whether or not we live well is all in our minds. Therefore, when people are of their original nature and are not saturated with false materiality, that is to say, when they are not in the material world, they do not feel discontent or in wanting. Instead they will live doing their best as they have the wisdom of knowing the law of 'cause and effect.' They will also be better off financially because they know that they will have results according to the efforts they make. Recovering one's original nature is the only way to have a better life through the wisdom gained, have a harmonious and comfortable social life, earn more money, and be blessed.

Without the original nature, one has a false mind and

lives as a slave to that mind. He does not know how to adapt to the world and just insists that the world does not fit his perspective. His mind is negative and does not have Truth, so for him living is difficult. The original nature is the never-dying world. When one recovers his original nature, knows the reason and purpose as to why he came to this world and becomes and lives with the original nature, then he will no longer pursue a good life for his body, for himself, but live for others. Wouldn't this be heaven on earth, a place where everyone can live well for there is no separation between 'you' and 'I' and everyone is 'me'? Such a place would be our kingdom, where we may all live well together. Only after recovering one's original nature, through what is the complete education, should people be educated in knowledge for their respective fields of endeavors. Right now people do not trust but hate each other, seek success by stepping on each other, and stubbornly claim that others are wrong, kill others, steal other's possessions, and think that only they are the best; this world is full of hypocrisy and lies. This is the way this world is. We can live exciting lives when we know the meaning and value of living for others by being educated on how to recover our original nature.

# The Wise One

A wise person is one with true wisdom

A person with wisdom can see himself

To see oneself means to see one's true self

It is also about knowing

That he has the false self within him

A wise person is one

Who knows his true self

Who knows the laws of the universe

He knows the laws of the world

He knows his self which is the origin

In fact, he knows everything

# Human Life I

Blue sky

Blue mountains and rivers

Through which jade water flows

Many bitter human feelings and grudges

Would have existed in these mountains and rivers


Who blamed who?

Who killed who and who saved who?

Only the sky knows

But the sky is silent


Human Life

Is absent of freedom

That life is an endless road without a destination

What do people live for?

Why do they live?

Why do they exist?

Man grows older and older fleetingly

Without knowing the reason


It is like walking through an endless dessert alone

It is a lonely and forlorn road

That continues on and on without a path


When one has Truth within

Truth exists within

He is the master

For he has the universe within him

There is no loneliness or solitude

There is no coming or going

Everything is 'me' as it is


People busily continue along in a roadless dessert

However, there is no true road

There is no destination

Thus without finding the water of life

Which is an oasis

They die

# One Who Is Born On The Earth Lives On The Earth
# One Who Is Born In Heaven Lives In Heaven

---

The sounds of birds, the sounds of animals

The sounds of the wind, the sounds of everything

The sounds of humans

All are the sounds of heaven

Sound comes from the shape


People have their own language

People have different regional languages

Humans along with the whole of creation

Come from heaven and live in heaven

But because humans do not have heaven in their minds

They live on the earth

One who is born on the earth lives on the earth

One who is born in heaven lives in heaven


One whose body and mind

Are reborn as the body and mind of heaven

Lives in heaven

One who just has his own body and mind

Lives on the earth

When one cleanses his body and mind – his self – and

When that self is no more

When the universe becomes his self

The universe is within him

One who has heaven lives in heaven

Which is the kingdom of heaven

Which is the forever-living, never-dying kingdom

Because it is the living soul and spirit of Truth

It is everlasting and never-dying

# What Is Rebirth And Resurrection?
# What Is Heaven?

People think that rebirth and resurrection are for body, the flesh, to be reborn and resurrected. They also think that heaven is someplace above. But all this is an illusion of conception. To be reborn is to be born again and to be resurrected also means the same thing – that the dead comes to life. Man's consciousness is not true but is his delusional conception and behaviors; it is false. Man's consciousness does not have life, and it is falseness that does not exist. Such consciousness is that which they have in their minds according to what they have learned; it is the whole of experiences from their lives which have passed; it has neither everlasting life nor does it have life, because it is not Truth.

Only Truth, which is everlasting and never-changing, is life itself.

When one's consciousness is awakened and alive, then there is life. Rebirth and resurrection are when one has the consciousness of Truth. That living consciousness of Truth is the sky – the emptiness of the universe, which is the state before all creations were born. This itself is the soul and spirit. Rebirth and resurrection are when one is reborn as this soul and spirit.

Heaven is the kingdom of Truth where one who is reborn as the soul and spirit of Truth lives. It is the kingdom where each and every creation is living.

In the kingdom of heaven every creation is reborn as the soul and spirit of the original universe. Therefore, the individual and the whole are one. There is no death in this kingdom. It is a living kingdom where the soul and spirit of all creations, Truth, lives. It is the forever-living, never-dying kingdom of the universe. It is the kingdom where only those who are reborn as that universe can live. Existence and non-existence are one and in that kingdom all existences live as the true existence.

The meaning of, 'one who is born in heaven lives in heaven,' is that one who has become the soul and spirit of heaven lives because he has the soul and spirit of heaven within. Everything is living and all are alive in the kingdom of Truth; but in man's falseness, everything is dead. Rebirth is to cleanse the falseness and be born as the soul and spirit of Truth.

Heaven is the kingdom within the mind, the soul and spirit. It is the kingdom where the body and mind of humans become one with the Creator of the universe. One who has this kingdom within him is Truth, which thus means that he is one who has gone to heaven. The material world is a limited existence, but the kingdom of the soul and spirit which is Truth, is the living kingdom of the Creator, which existed before the beginning, exists now, and will exist after eternity.

# The Soul And Spirit Is The Living Creator, Truth

When the day is clear and bright

And only the sky exists

We can see the sky well

Likewise

When your mind is clear

When you see the light, God

You can clearly see the world of the mind, Truth

Just as you will know Truth when you become Truth

Only one who becomes God

Can know God

Only one who becomes God

Can see God

Only one who becomes God

Lives the life of God

This universe is the land of God

This universe is the living land

But because people have not become God

And they are not living

They do not and cannot see the land of God

They cannot live there

The soul and spirit is the living Creator, Truth

It is the living existence, which exists as it is

It existed before the beginning,

And exists after eternity

One who is reborn as this God

In this kingdom of God

Is God

His soul and spirit is

The soul and spirit which is heaven

One who is reborn as heaven, Truth, lives there

Everything is one

But because people have not become the one soul and spirit

They live with their minds

Contained in every individual thing

# What Frightens The Devil The Most

The devil is

The copious number of false minds

Within oneself

The devil stays in the mind

And comes forth from time to time

Humans speak and act with that devil mind

For example

If there is someone you hate

When you meet that person

The mind of hatred comes forth

And you become the devil of hatred

If there is someone you love

When you meet that person

The mind of loving comes forth

And you become the devil of love

Pretending to know

Pretending to be something one is not

Pretending that it is so

Pretending to be superior

Pretending to be benign

Pretending to be good

Pretending to be kind

Pretending to be inferior

Pretending that it is not so

Pretending to be gentle

Pretending to be polite

Pretending to be scared

Pretending to have dignity

Pretending to be intelligent

To pretend is the false mind

That false mind is the devil

When you do not have pretence in the mind

You live well

When you do not have the devil of pretence

It is Truth

What frightens the devil the most

Are the words, 'I'm sorry' and 'thank you'

People live thinking they have done no wrong

But the person who is most at fault in the world

Is yourself, the devil


'Wrongdoing' from Truth's point of view

Is to not become Truth

That one is sorry, that one has wronged

Means to whole-heartedly enshrine Truth within

That man has not done so

Is his wrongdoing

When you say, 'I'm sorry; I have wronged'

Only Truth, the kingdom of Truth, exists

Therefore, the devil is expelled; it flees


Only the mind of God can say, 'I'm sorry; I have wronged'

When you think you are right,

Then it is your self-righteous devil which has come forth

But when you say, 'I'm sorry; I have wronged'

The devil dies

Because there is only Truth

# The True World

For I am compassionate

No matter who I meet, my mind does not fluctuate

I always treat people with compassion

I am always of that mind

Even in the past

I treated people to drinks without expectations

That compassion was always there

I never lost that compassion at any moment

I never hated or disliked

Although people are busy living for their own well-being

They have done nothing

Nothing remains, nothing has been achieved

Only more sighs and more agony

As time passes, that which they had in their minds long ago

Have also been forgotten

And though they become busier and busier

They are trapped in their own prisons, which they have made

And their minds become narrower

As their self-centered minds become more concrete

They had never been able to have

Any of the numerous things of existence

But only hollowness in their minds as they age

People live in this world

Unable to understand the laws of nature at all

Dazed in their false minds with dead eyes and dead ears

Although there is no place to go

They live only for themselves

A life that is meaninglessness itself

But it seems

The reason they have yet to awake from these dreams of theirs

Is because they do not know it is a dream for they are still in it

I have returned to the human world, the dream world

From the world beyond

I see that though everything in this world is a dream

People do not know this

While they are in this dream world

Although I talk about the new world

People who have never been to the new world

Do not know the new world

And cannot hear the story of the new world

And just speak of crazy, delusional things

Even though the time of harvest has come

People do not know

I tell them that this false world will come to an end

And that 'I' am the master of the true world

The undying world of freedom

I ask us all to go and live there

But immature humans do not listen to my words

I keep on telling them out of compassion

Which I have had since long ago

But nobody in the world listens to me

They listen to me and see me with their minds of the past

They do not understand me

Because they do not have the new world

The life of the new world within them

And because they have never been there

Leave this world behind

Where there is pain, burden, no freedom, and worries

Let us go to the new world where life is better

I am not a distinguished person

Nor am I so unfortunate

So it is only natural that people do not know

That the true world

Which is ordinary but extraordinary and perfect

Fits to my nature and is thus my world

Do not look at me, who I know is uncomely

Though the true, living, eternal and everlasting God

Cannot be seen

It is my nature, my wisdom itself

Thus one must become Truth and go to the new kingdom

In order to know this

Leave behind all yearnings, compassion, hatred, sighs

Bitter feelings and desires

Come with me, come with me to the kingdom of Truth

That life is of continuous suffering because it indeed is that life

Let us go in haste

To the living, perfect kingdom, the eternally living kingdom

Where existence lives forever as existence

A person who has a mind that resembles me has this kingdom

A person whose mind is reborn as my mind has this kingdom

As both the body and mind are the mind

There is the soul and spirit within that mind

Only a person who is reborn as that soul and spirit will live

To those who cry for compassion

For love, for blessings, for life

To those who cry because of bitter feelings

Because of their hatred of the world

Because of religion

Because of worries

Because they have or do not have

Because they do not have this and that

Because of their failure to achieve

Because of their failed dreams and desires

Because of not knowing the principles of nature

To those who want to know

To those who want to be enlightened and be perfect

To those who want to go to eternal heaven while living

All who are reborn as the new body and mind

Will live in the new world and live as the new world

Then they will know everything and achieve everything

Foolish-looking I may be

But what I am saying might actually be true

# In The Land Of Reality

In the darkness of the night

The wind makes a sound

I think someone had come

But tonight there is no one who will come to see me

There is no one looking for me

I look outside with hope

But no one is there

As I rest my head upon my pillow and look up at the ceiling

Millions of thoughts come to mind

Dreams about a glamorous life

Dreams about a fantasy world

But when morning comes

The dreams are far from reality

They are mere tales, like mere bubbles


Amidst insufficiency, people want to accomplish

Amidst insufficiency, people seek

The hungry look for food

The cold look for warm clothes

During times of poverty people dream of wealth

The powerless look for power

But all are empty dreams

Regardless of whether or not you achieve these

However in the land of reality

You can have all

And accomplish all

# Memories

The sun goes down over the western hill

The crescent moon is in the sky

Frogs in the field croak tirelessly

After a hard day's work

Everyone returns to their homes to have supper

Exhausted, they sleep


Adults gather with adults

Talking about the crops and farming

Youngsters gather with youngsters

Those of similar age and friends gather together

And lads and lasses meet together in secret


After years had passed, I visited that place of my past

No one from the past is there

All have left

Even the place has changed

Thoughtless dogs in the village bark

And though I meet an old acquaintance

The geniality of the past has gone; he has just become old

Only to the unknowing youngsters am I a guest

The memories remain within me

But those are futile illusions

Humans live off of their memories

And their past memories become their selves

Living off of the memories they have stored in their minds

# The Land That Lives In My Mind

Your mind is not clear

Your mind is not big

So you cannot see what is in your mind

You see and judge the world

With a mind that is not clear and big

With a mind in which you have stored numerous things

This is not judging with a righteous mind

It is just your own viewpoint

It is your own self-centered mind

It is your opinion and past experiences

Because this mind is not clear and big

What remains is a mind that is of the same shape as yourself

When you do not have that mind

When you have only the original mind

And when you become that original mind

You can see well what is in your mind

When you become the original mind

Nothing exists in the original mind but the sole God

Nothing exists, but God exists

The absence of all creations in the universe is the body

And in it there is the mind which is God

The whole of creation is

The appearance of the body and mind of God

All shapes are

The embodiment of both the soul and spirit in the mind

Existence is non-existence and non-existence is existence

All are one living soul and spirit

When the creator created the heaven and earth

And all creations

The creator created all as the living soul and spirit

However people are dead in their conceptions and behaviors

Because their minds are not clear and big

People cannot live

Without being reborn as the original mind

When I look upon the universe with its clear and big mind

The universe is living; the universe is in me

Because the universe is in me

I know all nature's laws

I know everything

# chapter three

## Human Completion

# Stories And Real Life

Old stories are

Just stories

Just illusions

Many stories are handed down

Many stories are told

But they are indeed just stories

The human mind has made such stories seem real

But they are not real

They are merely what the mind has made

Countless stories are totally false

Countless stories are totally meaningless

They are useless because they are not real


Old stories

Are mere stories now

And will continue to be mere stories in the future

Stories and what really exists are different

Stories are nothing more than just stories

That which really lives is real

Likewise, everything which really exists

Exists as it is

Those who know this

Are those who know the difference

Between stories and real life

Knowing is for those

Who have become Truth, who have become real

A true person knows that stories are false

He has awakened from the stories

Those who live in the illusions

Of made-up stories

Should awaken from their dream

And come out into the true world and live


In the true world there are no stories of illusions

In the true world all live life as it is

Without human resentment and bitterness

Without hatred or love, without likes or dislikes

It is the world

Without false stories

False words

Or false dreams


When humans live in the bright world

He becomes the bright world itself

He lives as one with the world

So thus he live a life of seeing as it is

And living as it is

He who becomes the universe

Lives in the universe with the universe in him

He lives life according to nature's flow without his false mind

He lives like wind; he lives like water

Only he who lives a life of nature by becoming nature itself

Knows what stories really are

# A Fine Mind

The mind should be fine

When the mind is unclean

It is not fine but coarse

It is a muddle of this and that

A coarse mind has many conflicts

To have many conflicts means that

Life is difficult

Happiness, wealth, fame are only for a fine mind

There is only unhappiness for one with a coarse mind

A person whose mind is unclean

Has many ups and downs of what is good and what is bad

But a fine mind has no such undulations

Anything can be contained in that mind

He who has a fine mind is a pure-hearted person

He who has a fine mind is a person whose mind is wide like the sea

He who has a fine mind can accept everything

He who has a fine mind has only the mind of Truth

Only the mind of Truth is a fine mind

# It Exists Because It Exists In The Mind

Should one blame others?

Should one blame the world?

Should one blame his ancestors, his parents, or his family?

All just exist as they are and live as they are

But one's mind has not become the world

Thus many things remain as bitter feelings

Exist as bitter feelings

Because his mind exists

Because the world does not fit his mind

Bitter feelings exist because they exist in one's mind

Because things do not fit his mind

If one no longer has bitter feelings in his mind

Then he no longer has any bitter feelings altogether

Only a person who has become

The mind of Truth, the original nature

Has no false mind at all

He lives the life of true nature, he lives like nature

Everything exists in one's mind

# Darkness And Brightness

What are you going to do when the morning comes?

What are you going to do when a new day brightens?

One who is afraid of the brightness of the day

Is afraid because his mind is dark

A dark-minded person does not like the bright of day

But likes the darkness

When you do not have brightness

But have darkness, in your mind

It is difficult to have a bright mind

You hide in the darkness

And do not want to be bright

You can work properly

Only when the day is bright

You can live and work righteously

Only when your mind is bright

# Humans Are Ghosts

To all people:

Though they look like human beings

There is no Truth in the shape of man

Thus, man acts like a ghost

Humans who live with ghosts

Live not knowing they are ghosts

But humans who are not ghosts

Can see ghosts

Ghosts are the delusions of one's mind

And since people live not with a true mind

But with countless ghosts in their minds

They themselves become their minds of ghosts

And live as those ghosts

This ghost for this situation and that ghost for that situation

They live with a ghost for every occasion

Though they look like human beings, man is a ghost

When he is angry, he is a ghost of anger

When he has hatred, love, jealousy, and an enemy

He is that ghost

When he laughs, he is a ghost of laughter

This is because his mind is the ghost

Man stores non-existent things in his mind

And lives the life of a ghost, a life which is not righteous

A righteous person is one who has a mind of Truth

When a person lives with that mind

He is righteous

He is living

Ghosts are illusions of the dead

A righteous one is the trueness of a living person

# How To Educate People So That They May Become Complete

The purpose of education is to make people complete. We define a complete and well-rounded person as one who has knowledge, virtue, physical ability, and artistic abilities. In China it means to have benevolence, knowledge, and courage. We say that a complete person is the one who is intelligent, benevolent, and courageous; but one does not become such a person by merely repeating those words.

A complete person is a perfect person without any insufficiencies. A complete person is one who has become Truth itself and knows what is true through wisdom. A complete person is love itself and has great mercy and compassion; he lives a life of nature with a mind of nature. Such a person is one who has accomplished all. Therefore, without becoming the forever-living, never-dying God, one cannot be a complete person. Through religion, ideology, philosophy, countless people have tried for many years to become this perfect existence, but have failed. This is because they do not know what this existence actually is, nor do they have the method of becoming this existence. The purpose of education today is to teach people how to make a living. And even though there are studies of religion, ideology and philosophy, people just memorize these teachings, not knowing that they cannot become Truth, the perfect existence, by memorizing and storing such things in their minds; thus they will never be able to see or become this perfect existence of Truth. When a person is completely free of his self-centered conceptions and behaviors, when he is reborn as the true existence, which is the never-dying universe itself, he can become a truly complete person.

We are frequently told to, 'love your enemies,' 'have compassion,' 'be merciful' and 'be virtuous.' We pretend to follow these words, but there is nobody who truly does. The only person who can love the enemy is God, Truth. Only God can give great mercy, compassion and benevolence.

In Korea, there is a saying, "Everything turns out according to how I have made up my mind." This does not mean one can be rich if he just wishes to earn a lot of money. It means that one's life will only be in accordance with what one has in his mind. Each person's mind is different depending on what he has stored in his mind, which has no shape. Therefore one who has learned computer skills since childhood will have computers in his mind, for which he can earn a living by using them. This is because, though the mind has no form, he has computers in his mind. If he had learned law he would make a living with that. If he has medicine in his mind, he could live in accordance with that. People live by what they have in their minds; they live only as much as they have in their minds, no more, no less.

Humans blame others, placing fault on others for everything. However, the way they live now is due to their own selves. In Korea people say, "Everything bad that happens is due to my ancestors; everything good that happens is due to my merit." But it seems they live in this world, failing to realize that everything that happens, good or bad, is due to oneself. Do not live in this world with heavy, painful burdens. When you live truly by becoming a complete person, there is freedom and liberation; you can live well for you have great wisdom. When everyone becomes complete, then religion, ideology, philosophy, and education will become one. When everybody becomes complete, this world will be heaven and this world will be a good place to live in. Without being reborn as God, Truth, people cannot become complete.

The true existence is the pure emptiness of the universe beyond the universe. This existence existed before eternity and will exist after eternity. It is endless without beginning or end. It is the living existence, which exists as it is and on its own. This is the Creator itself and is the existence which every religion believes in. Unless our bodies and minds are reborn as the body and mind of the universe, the Creator, we cannot become complete. What people know is only the experience they have gained from their lives. They live with heavy burdens because they live holding onto the shadows of their lives.

The way to become Truth – the Creator of this infinite universe – is to subtract both one's self and the universe from the universe. Then only the everlasting, never-dying Creator remains. When you subtract your body, mind and even the universe from this universe, you can see and become the true God. This is the method of Maum Meditation and the method to become a complete person. People live painful lives holding onto shadows. But you must erase those shadows, in order to become Truth, live in heaven, and be a complete person.

Since their childhood, people accumulate numerous minds within, but they have never cleansed those minds. Those minds reside heavily within each cell of their bodies causing their 'chi (energy)' and blood to not circulate properly. This often causes numerous diseases. We can often witness how diseases are naturally eliminated when such minds of shadows are cleansed. We see how comfortable, beautiful and bright people become when their delusional minds disappear from their faces. When one's entire body is the soul and spirit of the universe, then he is a complete person. When his mind is enlightened by the fact that he is the everlasting, never-dying universe, he is a perfect person. Many people seek Maum Meditation because such enlightenment is achieved through the method of Maum Meditation. That is why Maum Meditation flourishes all over the world.

# Our Bodies Should Be Reborn As The Perfect Mind Of Truth

---

The clouds are sleeping

The clouds are sleeping silently

I am the cloud; there is nothing that is not me

The skies of America are very clear

The skies of Korea are saturated with pollution and dark

Because of the yellow sand storms blowing in from China

The skies of America are so blue that it is almost dark

Now that my mind has become the sky

It is neither dark nor blue but empty

And in the empty sky there is nothing but the sole God


This God exists as it is

And is the state

Before the wind, the cloud, and the whole of creation

Everything is God

The material and non-material are one

Humans know only what is material

And do not realize

That non-material existence is the real material existence

Everything that exists is non-material existence

Though nothing may exist, material existence exists

Though nothing may exist, non-material existence exists

People do not know this existence

Because they do not have this existence in their minds

This existence is the master of the whole universe

And the origin of all creations

However, no one knows this


I have become this existence

And work for the kingdom of this existence

I live with wisdom

People have to accumulate their own blessings

I have accumulated a wealth of blessings

But people do not have such blessings

To be completely enlightened

Is to become one with the sole God of the empty sky

And be reborn

In order to become completely one with this existence

One must have the spirit of this existence in his mind

Also one's self must no longer exist

And be the sole God of the empty sky

One's whole body must become

The spirit and light of the universe

One must realize that

He has become the perfect existence itself


Though 'I' know nothing

And live as it is

'I' am the eternal Truth

That lacks nothing

'I' am the God of wisdom

And live doing the work of heaven

# The Biggest, Widest, Lowest, And Highest Existence In The World

There are many things in the world, and everything in the world can be seen by human eyes. However, there is one thing that people do not know even though they see it. It is image of the Creator. The image of the Creator who created the universe is the original image of the universe. People call this existence the emptiness or the sky. There is no one who knows what the Creator really is because people have their self-centered minds which are as big as their selves. A complete person is one who knows and becomes this existence. Because humans have a self-centered mind they separate every creation, including themselves, from the Creator and they live within their own delusional universe.

We all know that countless forms were created from this universe. The stars of the universe came forth from this infinite universe as did the sun, moon, Earth, along with every creation on Earth and every human being on Earth. The universe consists of the divine soul and spirit of God, and it is divinity that brings forth everything. Everything is born from harmony, and that harmony is the condition that brings forth everything.

A condition is the cause that enables a material existence to appear. Everything that comes forth is the representation of the body and mind of the universe. This colossal universe is made up of the colossal soul and spirit. Even though the shape of everything is different, everything is the representation of this great soul and spirit. The shape is the soul, and the mind within the shape is the spirit.

Every single creation on Earth comes forth according to condition, the harmony of the universe; and everything that has appeared should simply be the great soul and spirit, but people are distanced from great soul and spirit because of their self-centered minds. This great soul and spirit is the everlasting, never-dying Truth. It existed before eternity and will exist after eternity; it is a living existence. But people cannot see and become this existence because they do not have the true soul and spirit in their minds due to their delusions, due to the minds of their shapes. This is because their minds have not become the infinite universe, because their minds are not born as the soul and spirit of Truth. This is what it means to be dead and trapped in one's own delusional tomb.

Delusion is not real but false. People live false lives because they do as the falseness within them orders. But even though they live false lives, they do not know it is false because they are within that false life. People do not know they are dreaming in their dream, and only come to realize that the dream is false once they have awakened from the dream. Similarly, when people have only the experiences of their past in their minds, they think that that is Truth. They think that that is all there is and thus live in their tombs.

When one becomes the living existence of Truth, which is the biggest, widest, lowest, and highest infinite Creator, he is one who has awakened from his dream because he knows that he was dead and trapped in hell. Liberation means to be free from one's own false conceptions and behaviors. It is to become Truth, the infinite universe, and to be born as the child of the universe. This is liberation and freedom for one no longer has his false self. Such an existence exists as it is, without conflict, without hindrance, without life and death. When one returns to the infinite universe which will never disappear no matter what, one's delusional self will die and he will be born again as the existence of Truth; this is Maum Meditation.

When one discards both his false mind and his body, which is his self, and also discards the universe, then Truth remains. Then once one completely discards his self to Truth itself, only Truth remains. Because people have soiled minds, they thus have minds that need to be cleansed; such soiled minds are sin. A person whose sin is absolved can be one with the Creator. Not becoming one with Truth is the only sin there is. In order to become one with the infinite universe, the Creator, you must throw away your mind of attachment, which is yourself. Throwing away the countless things within your self-centered mind and being reborn as the infinite universe is Maum Meditation. When everybody is free from their false self-centered minds and is reborn as complete Truth, then oneness will be fulfilled on this earth. They will forever live on this earth as Truth with the blessings they have accumulated in heaven. And only those who know this will feel sorry for those who do not. People live in this world according to what they have within their minds. The person who has Truth within his mind will live with Truth and live eternally with the blessings he has gathered in the kingdom of Truth.

# The Will Of God

The will of God

Is the empty mind

Free from everything

Because God is living

God's will is to make heaven, humans, and the earth live

For God, completion is

To make every existing creation God itself

And make all creations live forever

As the energy and light in the kingdom of God

This is the will of God

The master of the kingdom of God is

The person who has become God, and who has Truth within

A true life is possible because humans exist

Without humans there is no meaning or significance

One who becomes God is the master

By the will of the one who becomes God

Heaven, the kingdom of God, is built

He who becomes God

Will accumulate his blessings in the kingdom of God

And will live forever with his blessings

By the will of man

Heaven, earth and humans live

By the will of man

A new heaven and earth is created

The human mind sees man and God as being separate

However, man and God are one and completion, itself

# The Creator Is A Living Existence, The Existence Which Lives As It Is

The Creator gives birth to everything in the universe and is the master of everything in the universe. This existence is the great soul and spirit of the universe. It is the omnipotent and omniscient existence. Omnipotence is within the domain of the soul, and omniscience is within the domain of the spirit. It is the living entity and exists as it is. It existed before eternity and exists after eternity. It does not have death, and it is the mother and father of all creations in the universe as well as the master. The whole of creation is the representation of this entity. The whole of creation is the existence of this entity. It is omnipotent because it brings forth all creations, and it is omniscient because it knows all is one and alive.

We call this existence Tao, God, Haneolim, Buddha, Allah, true nature, true mind, the origin, the original mind, Truth, Creator, Divinity, Soul and Spirit, Body and Mind of Buddha, Holy Ghost and Holy Father, and the body and mind of the universe.

This existence is the universe before the great universe.

The soul is the existence that has nothing, while the spirit is the existence which exists amidst that nothingness. All creations in the universe are one with the soul and spirit of this existence and are living. However, man is dead, trapped in his false mind. Because this existence is living, every living thing in the universe lives by the will of the body and mind of God. Man must also return to this existence in order to achieve human completion, live eternally and be in heaven.

The Creator and the whole of creation in the universe are one, and all creations are the children of the Creator. This existence is oneness itself and is living; thus this universe is already awakened and the kingdom of God is already saved. However, man is dead and lives with pain and burden because he is not one with this Creator. Though the human body lives on the energy from food, it does not have a real life unless he becomes the energy and light of the Creator, God, Truth.

The universe is alive. Likewise, man can also live forever when his mind has become Truth, and only when he lives with that mind can he live forever. The existence of this Creator is the forever-living existence without death because it is Truth. No one in this world can live without being reborn as the child of this existence.

The ultimate purpose of all religions is eternal life in the forever-living kingdom of heaven. This purpose will come to fruition when we offer up our selves and become one with the Creator. In the kingdom of this existence, there is no death and only this existence lives there. When humans are reborn by being absolved from their sins, then all religions will be completed and it will be the time when humans become the owner. Since the original Creator created all things in the universe, it is also the responsibility of the Creator to make them live. Only by the blessings of the Creator can humans and all things in the universe live.

Since Earth has one Sun
Each location has its season
However, there is spring, summer, fall and winter
If one place is cold, then another place is hot
And there are also places that have
Pleasant temperatures and are nice to live
As people live in this world
They blame the world and resent the world

Because of the minds they have

But one who becomes the world

Lives with gratitude


That this exists and that exists

Is all possible because the world exists

When one returns to

The origin of the profoundness of that world

And the preciousness of existence

And when one has gratitude for

The value of that existence and gratitude for principles

Then everything is one with 'me'

Yet, everything exists on its own

# What Is The Mind?

---

Each and every creation has its own shape, which is its mind.
All creations live according to their shapes. For centuries,
people have studied the mind and tried to define its identity of
the mind. But no one has ever been able to explain its accurate
meaning and define it; nor does anyone know it is that should
be emptied from the mind.

In the Bible, it says, "Blessed are the poor in spirit for
theirs is the kingdom of heaven." Likewise, although it has
been said that we need to empty and cleanse our mind, our
spirits, we do not know what that mind is that needs to be
cleansed. No one knows the existence of that mind and the
shape of that mind; nor does anyone know what the mind is.

The original mind is the universe before the infinite
universe. That universe is Truth, energy and light, and existed
before eternity and will exist after eternity. It is the forever-
living, never-dying God, and all creations in the universe are
the representation of this existence, for which they are this
existence, itself. The origin of all creation is the sky before the

sky. The universe before the universe – the Creator, the great soul and spirit of the universe – is the mother and father of all creation; it is our origin, our original minds. This existence is always alive and is both the energy and light of Truth. Therefore it is the omnipotent and omniscient existence that has no death.

The reason and purpose of finding our original minds is to live forever and to live in heaven where there is no death. Even when everything in this world disappears, this existence lives forever as it is. It is energy and light, the origin of the great universe. A person who is reborn as this energy and light of the universe can live.

People live with the energy from food for their bodies while they are alive. But when one is reborn as the energy and light of the great universe – the soul and spirit of the great universe – while living, he will not die even though his material body passes away. Man will have no death once he is reborn with the true mind by cleansing his mind.

People's minds are different according to their shapes. This is because as soon as he is born in to this world in the likeness of his parents' shapes, his mind is different according to his shape. People are sinners because they are not one with Truth. They have original sin because they inherited their bodies from their parents who are also sinners.

Humans have both a body and a mind. And that mind lives according to its shape, which is original sin. In their shapes, people store self-centered minds, along with the shadows of the memories from throughout their lives; such is what becomes one's false self. They live believing that what the delusional false self of attachments commands is indeed one's self. Humans live exactly as much as they have stored in their minds, no more, no less. For example, if you have store knowledge about medicine in your mind, you work with medicine; if you have stored legal knowledge in your mind, then you live working in the field of law. Throughout their lives, people only store this and that in their minds, but never cleanse those minds. Therefore, man has become a slave to his own mind, living with painful burden and agony. Man's mind is not one but billions of minds, and thus his mind changes day and night. In order to cleanse your false mind to find the true mind, you must discard the false life that you have lived, your false body that contains your false mind, as well as the false universe; then only the true mind will remain.

The true mind is Truth, the great soul and spirit, and the body and mind of Truth. When you are reborn as this soul and spirit you will live righteously without death. When this land, here, becomes the forever-living heaven, you can live in heaven even when your body dies. The mind you must cleanse is the self-centered false mind; and once you throw away that self-centered mind, your body that contains that mind, along with the universe you have in your false self, then the mind of Truth remains, and you will be reborn as the mind of Truth. This is Maum Meditation. Maum Meditation is about cleansing one's false self because everything is one's own fault, not the fault of others. The entire practice of Maum Meditation is about discarding one's self so that one no longer exists, and thus being born again as the existence of Truth.

# When You Become Truth

When you become Truth

There is no mind of self

When everybody returns to the original mind of Truth

This world will become one

Because everybody is of one mind

Their minds do not change

They are wisdom itself, they live with one mind

There is no separation of 'you' and 'me'

There is no 'your country,' 'my country'

There is no 'your religion,' 'my religion'

Everybody will go to heaven while living

Everybody will live the life of heaven

They will do everything, following nature's law

They will do everything with trueness

And will thus have a perfect plan

They will live following that perfect plan

All humans will be complete

All will live for others with one mind

# Blessings

People complain that they have no blessings. They say that they are not blessed in terms of their parents, spouse, children, or finances; and they complain about their lives. Countless people live with countless different matters of life. A blessing means to find the place which speaks of oneness. In other words, it means to see the place that speaks of Truth, which is oneness.

People speak and act to the extent of what they have in their minds. Therefore only when they have blessings in their minds are they blessed. Those who do not have blessings in their minds envy other people's fortune. People will live and have as many blessings in the world as they have within their minds. A person who does not have those blessings in his mind will live without it.

What currently determines one's actions and spoken words is his mind within. Therefore people who do not have blessings in the mind are not blessed because they cannot accept blessings and only reject them. You cannot earn money just by thinking and talking about earning money. But rather you will earn just as much as your mind is prepared to accept and act. What determines one's actions is his mind, and thus people live accordingly, no more, no less. As I meet more and more people, I find that many people have closed minds, and therefore they do not have blessings.

Those who have an open mind can accept and contain everything. Therefore, they can contain blessings. No matter what they do, people with big minds will be successful without conflicts and hindrances as they work and behave without their frames of mind, which are their selves. People who try to fit the world into their own selfish minds will find the world disagreeable. When their minds become as big as the world, they can understand the world and fit into it. People who do not have Truth in their minds cannot accomplish anything because their minds change all the time; and even though their minds are busy they achieve nothing. But the minds of those who have a foundation of Truth are not busy; their actions match their words, for which they can gain as much as they have done; thus they live righteous and successful lives.

We can commonly see people praying for blessings, but there is no room in their minds for blessings. In other

words, they have narrow minds, and their minds are not big
enough and are not a true existence. Blessings will reside
only in those who have a big mind, who have a clean mind.
Moreover, blessings come from one's actions, and those actions
come from their minds. Therefore, when people truly cleanse
their minds and are reborn as Truth, they will have their
worldly blessings as well. The biggest blessing in the world for
man is to become complete and live eternally. A person with
true blessings will not expect blessings for him but accumulates
true blessings for others.

Blessings do not come when you ask or beg for it,
but blessings are something we build like we build a house.
When you accumulate your blessings in the kingdom of your
true mind, you will live forever with those blessings in the
everlasting true land. One who does not have blessings in his
mind expects blessings, while one who has blessings in the
mind accumulates blessings. Blessings do not come to one who
expects blessings for he expects them through his false mind.
But one who accumulates his blessings will build his blessings
and everything he does will be a blessing.

# Trueness In The Mind

People speak only of what they have in their minds

And live acting according to what they have in that minds

People who have Truth in their minds

Live as Truth in the kingdom of Truth

Because they have Truth

Only people who have Truth know Truth

And live doing the deeds of Truth

Everything is Truth

All live in the completed kingdom of Truth

They have no death because they have Truth in their minds

# Revelation

Not long ago, there was a book called, 'Conversations with God,' which was a bestseller in the U.S. Also there are some people who say that they have received revelations from God while praying in the mountains. However prior to this, people must first know what God is. God is the origin of all creations, and both the mother and father of all creations. God is the omnipotent and omniscient Creator. God is the universe before the universe, both body and mind of the universe. God exists in the emptiness where nothing exists. That emptiness is the body of the universe and God exists in it. People cannot see God because they do not have God in their mind due to their false minds.

People know, speak, and live according to what they have in their minds. What they have seen, heard, and learned are all stored within their minds. They live thinking that such things they have stored in their minds are knowledge. In order to have the widest, biggest, highest and lowest mind of the universe, we must cleanse both our bodies and minds and even the universe that is in our minds. People know as much as what they have within their mind, and likewise, people know God when God resides within their minds. This itself is the existence of Truth. Truth is the eternal, never-dying God.

There will be the world of God, the true world, when this world, which is hell, along with oneself of this world no longer exists. A person, who no longer has his self and is reborn as God, is God. When we talk about 'revelations from God,' the 'God' here seems to be similar to God, but since such revelations occur within one's own mind, it is not truly God. True God cannot be known through revelations, but through wisdom; this is Truth.

Conversations with God are actually the sounds of one's own false mind, and the revelations received through prayer is also the same. As time passes, such things are results of one's greed. Such things occur in one's own mind. And when people say they can read the minds of others, they are actually reciting what they have in their own minds.

A person who has been reborn with the body and mind of God knows through wisdom, and does not have revelations. When asked, "What is the reason for living? And

what is the purpose of life?" a person who has been reborn
will respond, "To live eternally," which has come to know
through wisdom. When asked, "Are there any descendents of
Truth?" one who has become Truth knows with wisdom that
everyone who becomes Truth is a child of God, one with God,
and God itself. When one is enlightened of all eight levels of
Maum Meditation, he is a complete person. If there are any
questions as to whether he is complete or not complete, then he
is not complete and is false. If he still has a false God who says
whether or not he is complete, then that is all false.

A person whose mind has been completely reborn
as Truth is one who has achieved completion; and he himself
knows that he has achieved completion. It is false to say
that some existence from heaven can make one complete.
Enlightenment is to know as much as one's mind has become
enlarged and cleansed. Only a person who is completely
enlightened of all eight levels will know what is false. Some
people say that there exists a fifth dimensional world or a
fourth dimensional world, but all of these are delusional
worlds. Only the perfect Truth exists in the true and perfect
world. This is the world of the eternal and never-dying God.

Only this world is the highest and the most perfect world of Truth. This world just exists as it is.

# Maum Meditation Is About Becoming Truth, The True Mind
## The Proof That One Has Become Truth Is...

The everlasting Truth is the eternal, never-dying God itself. The nature of Truth is that it is the living existence, which existed before the beginning and will exist after the end. It is the original shape of this vast universe. The original shape is the place of the Creator, which is the mother and father of all creation. It is the place before the whole of creation came forth and the place where everything comes from. It is the place where nothing exists but the sole God.

This place is without beginning or end and is the living existence which exists as it is. Nobody knows this existence because they do not have this existence within. People speak, behave, and live only as much as they have within their minds. When people become Truth while living and when there is the true kingdom within them, then he will have eternal life and heaven where life and death are the same.

When man discards his mind, his body as well as the universe in order to become the perfect existence of Truth, then only the origin of this universe remains. When one is reborn as this origin, then that kingdom is the kingdom of Truth, heaven; he is reborn as Truth. Human completion means to become Truth, to have no death, and to live as it is. But humans are not able to become this existence because they do not know or see this existence. The method for humans to completely become this existence is:

The complete Existence

 When one's self, the stars, the Sun, the Moon, and the Earth no longer exist in this universe...

...then only this complete existence remains.  This existence becomes one's mind.

The proof that one has been completely reborn as this existence is...

Truth, Soul and Spirit

The Soul and Spirit exist.

And one's mind is reborn as the spirit of Truth.

Humans only know and think according to what they have in their minds. Yet a person whose mind changes into and is reborn as the spirit of Truth, of the universe, is one with the universe because his spirit is one with the universe.

This is called becoming one with the spirit of the universe. When one is reborn as the soul and spirit, he realizes that everything in the universe is of one soul and spirit. He is reborn as the soul and spirit of Truth and becomes the mind of the true soul and spirit. He is a complete person as he is enlightened of his perfection.

Soul and Spirit

Truth

One whose mind has become the mind of the universe has the spirit of Truth.

One whose body becomes the body of the universe has the soul of Truth.

One who becomes the mind of Truth will be enlightened of his completion.

To be complete means to be Truth. Proof that one has Truth itself is:

1. He has become the spirit of Truth.

2. He has become the soul of Truth.

3. He is complete.

One who realizes all three of the above is one who accomplished everything; he is complete.

# The Life Of A Person Who Is Alive

He eats when it is time for him to eat

Sleeps when he is tired

When he laughs, when he drinks

When he rests, when he works

Even when he lives, he just lives as it is

While Truth just does

People do things by their false minds, not by Truth

Although these two things seem the same

It is the difference between being true and being false

Although they seem the same

It is the difference between being alive and being dead

It is the difference between the almighty Truth and the false

It is the difference between heaven and earth

It is the difference between life in hell and life in heaven

# Eternal Life

Now that night has fallen deep in the mountains

Where clouds and the winds come to sleep

The birds sleep

In the midst of the noises of animals

That can be heard from time to time

I feel humanly loneliness

Within the uninhabited mountains

There are trees, grass, and animals that are fit for that place

This place is their homes

Looking at the roads humans traveled in order to live

It seems they just busily treaded back and forth

What had been the purpose of their lives?

What had they lived for?

Though these are questions which are still yet to be solved

I can only assume that many people have already passed away

That man is born and that man lives

Is because he is born from the harmony of the universe

Lives by the harmony of the universe

And eventually passes on

According to the conditions of the universe

But those who have passed on are silent

And man does not have the wisdom in his minds

Thus, there is no one who knows the answer

That they have passed on means that

They followed their delusions because they did not have Truth

And went to the land of their delusions

They went to a land of hell

Only God of the universe

Can teach the way to live in the land of God

God has lived for a long, long while

And thus knows about all happenings of the universe

Only those who become God itself

Know about the laws of the world

When we see from their minds

Which have become the body and mind of the universe

We can see that the universe came forth

From the soul and spirit of that universe

The shape of God is every creation in the universe

Originally, everything in the universe was built perfectly

And every existing shape was alive, however,

Humans are dead

Because their consciousness are dead

And they are unable to become God

They do not have wisdom nor can they live

Because they are trapped in their minds

And cannot become God, Truth

If humans want to live, their selves must die

And be reborn as the consciousness of the Creator

If they are not reborn

They cannot live because they are not Truth

The Creator is the living existence

Every creation is born through cause and effect

And is thus the original Creator

Everything that those creations give birth to

Is actually created by the Creator

Every creation that appears is the child of the Creator

And is also one with the Creator

But humans cannot become one

Because of their conceptions and behaviors

Everyone is trapped in their frame of mind which is false

And will eventually die

The Creator, which is the body and mind of the universe

Is the place before material existence

It is not material but a non-material, real existence

No matter how small one material object may be

It cannot be smaller than this existence, and thus

This existence just exists as every shape in the universe

The body and mind of the universe

Is the Creator of material shape

And this body and mind exists on its own

Everything is the embodiment of this existence

And is this existence itself

Existence is non-existence and non-existence is existence itself

It is wholly oneness of the body and mind of the universe itself

When man's mind is reborn as the body and mind of Truth

The body and mind of Truth exists within him

He is the body and mind of Truth itself

He is everlasting and never-changing because he is Truth

He lives forever

# Conversations With God

People quite often say that God is a personal God. They say that God is inside us, and thus they create a 'god' in their minds who they supposedly have conversations with. But it is one's own mind, one's false, delusional mind, that is doing these things.

God is the soul and spirit itself – the soul and spirit, which is as big as the universe and which is the universe before the universe. God does not exist in man's mind because of man's sins. Man makes his own god according to his own standards and thinks God answers him in his mind. However that God is one's own delusional, false god; it is the god of one's own delusions. Thus the answers one receives are also the words of one's own mind; they are all false. In other words, all that one is promised, all the results one is assured when he had made his requests – as time passes, we come to find that nothing is achieved. We can only have God inside our minds when we are reborn as Truth. When man is reborn as the body and mind of the universe, which is the soul and spirit of Truth, then he is Truth for he is the child of Truth.

That one receives an answer from God means that God and oneself are separate. God is not like that. A person who is reborn as the soul and spirit, which is Truth, comes to know everything for he has wisdom. The book titled, 'Conversations With God' is about the answers received from one's own mind which have become 'God'; however, this means that one is possessed by the entity he thinks to be 'God'. Only a person who is reborn as a child of God, only a person who has God in him, and thus only a person who has seen God, will come to know everything through wisdom.

Originally, God does not have a shape but is the soul and spirit itself. The spirit is wisdom, which is the mind. When you are asked, "Why do humans live?" you will come to know the answer with wisdom, the answer being, "To live forever." When you are asked, "What is the method for humans to live forever?" you will come to know with wisdom that the answer is, "You cannot live forever without becoming Truth." In general, the 'God' one has in his is that of his mind. It is not the true God. The meaning of a 'personal God' is that God will appear as a human being. The origin of God of the holy soul and holy spirit must come as a human being so that there will be the Holy Son of God. Because humans cannot be reborn as Truth unless there is a true human. When you are reborn as Truth, you will have been born as a child of God, and thus you will see clearly your foolishness of your false mind having pretended to be God. Preachers who have such false 'Gods' have many followers because those followers do not know Truth and believe that such false 'Gods' are true.

God is the Creator – the Great Soul and Spirit before the great universe. This Creator brings forth everything because it is omnipotent and omniscient. Therefore, a person, born again as the body and mind of God, is the God of wisdom. He will know the laws and the will of the universe. However, humans mistakenly think that they know everything when in all actuality humans know only what they have experienced and learned. All of that is false. When his mind becomes the whole universe, the world, the Creator, he will know the laws and the will of the world.

The 'God' which one's delusions have created in his mind is a false God. The 'God' which is said to be inside us is the great soul and spirit, Truth of the universe beyond one's own mind. Only when you go to New York will you know New

York. Likewise, you will know this existence only when you become this existence. A person who becomes this existence will come to know the natural flow of the world through wisdom – not through revelations, not through answers.

# Resurrection

Will you go?

Or will you stay?

One who goes has no place to go

But one who stays seeks in his mind for a place to go

Within man's conceptions, heaven is a place far, far away

No one has taught them how to go to heaven because

Though many people talk about it, no one has been to heaven

When there is no coming or going

When only the man's mind grows bigger

And when man's mind has the world

Then the master of the world would be man

Man will be the owner of the world

It is the world for one who no longer has his own self

When one no longer has a mind and body of his own

And no false universe

Then that place becomes reality, the true world

That is the perfect place as there is no death

One whose body and mind are reborn as this perfect place

Will live eternally

This is resurrection

This is the new heaven and the new earth; it is the living

kingdom

# The True Meaning Of The Phrase, 'Jal Moshida'

Koreans say 'jal moshida' as a phrase meaning 'to be at fault.' Yet, the original meaning of the words 'jal moshida' is 'to have Truth within me.' 'Jal' is an adverb meaning 'very well' and 'very well' refers to the existence of Truth; 'moshida' means 'to have within and worship.' Therefore, the meaning of 'jal moshida' is 'to have Truth within and worship it.'

The Korean phrase, 'honjul nada,' is frequently used when one has gone through some sort of calamity, or when someone has had a near death experience or overcomes death. However, the original meaning of the word, 'honjul nada' is 'to be reborn as the mind of the universe'. 'Honjul' means 'the mind of the universe,' while 'nada' means 'to be born/reborn.' Therefore, the meaning of 'honjul nada' is 'to be reborn as the mind of the universe.' This means to have the mind of God, the mind of the universe. And this is why we use the phrase 'honjul nada' when we have overcome death.

Thus, the meaning of 'jal moshida' is, 'I apologize because I do not have Truth within me.' Also, it means, 'I will cleanse away the delusional evil mind by keeping Truth within me.'

# The Reason We Must Discard Our Minds Is Because Everything That Has Happened In The World And Everything That Exists In The World Are Delusions

What is it that you have in your mind?

If you continuously discard your false mind

You will no longer have your false body and mind

And only Truth will remain

Discarding the mind means

To discard everything that happened in the world

And discarding everything that exists in the world

For they are all false

# God's Mind

To have a mind means to have a self-centered mind

To have no mind means

To have no self-centered mind and to have only God's mind

God's mind is

An empty mind, free from human knowledge

That mind is emptiness itself and it exists as it is

It is free from knowledge because it knows everything

It is a state, free of human conceptions and behaviors

It is a state, which is absent of time and space, past and future

It is the state of one mind

It is the mind born again as the God of the universe

It is freedom, unbound to this or that

It is freedom without confinement

Because it is God of the universe itself

This is great freedom and liberation

It is great freedom, liberation and Truth

Because one's self no longer exists

The place where existence and non-existence are one

The place where non-existence and existence are one

The place of the origin of all creation

The place before all creation

That place is real

That place is Truth

That place is living

That place is the state of everlasting, never-dying energy

And the state of God

That place exists by itself

That place has always existed

That place exists as it is without beginning or end

It is the perfect place

It is perfect because it never dies

It is the place of the mother and father of all creation

It is the place of the master of all creation

It is the non-material true existence before material existence

Its nature is to exist but not exist

To not exist but to exist

Its dimensions are beyond material existence

It exists just as light exists – light which exists

Even though light is not a material existence

It exists even within a material existence of the smallest unit

It exists as it is

The meaning of 'to exist but not exist' is that

Although this existence exists

It does not exist in the sense it is not material

All creations are the embodiment of that existence

And the life of every creation is that existence

It is the omnipotent and omniscient soul and spirit

Omniscience is the spirit, the wisdom of God

Omnipotence is the soul that brings forth all creations

All creations in the world

Comes from the body and mind of this soul and spirit

The true meaning of omniscience is to know everything

To completely know Truth, the origin, is omniscience

To completely know reality, the origin, is omniscience

And to know the laws of the universe is omniscience

Truth creates every shape in this world; this is omnipotence

Every creation in the world

Is the representation of the life of Truth

# Light And Darkness II

You can see everything when it is daylight

But you cannot see anything when it is dark

Likewise, when you have your own mind within you

You cannot know the ways of the world

You will know the ways of the world

When you have true mind within you

The difference between

Having and not having the true mind within

It is the difference between true and false

It is the difference between light and dark

It is the difference between existence and non-existence

It is the difference between knowing and not knowing

It is the difference between life and death

It is the difference between heaven and earth

Heaven is already perfect and living

However, man's mind does not reach heaven

Therefore, there is no one who is living

People live life according to what they have in their minds

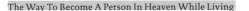

Likewise, only people who have heaven in their minds

Will live for as long as heaven lives, in heaven

# Are You Complete?

- Have you drunk the water from the fountain of life and thus forget your entire past?
- Have you been born again after having drunk the water of life?
- Has your mind become one with the spirit of Truth?
- Have your body and mind become one with the soul and spirit of Truth?
- Have you been enlightened of perfection?
- Have you accomplished all? Have you been enlightened of everything?
- Do you know everything? Are you complete?
- To have accomplished all, to have been enlightened of everything, to know everything is to be born again as Truth so as to live the life of heaven.

# Only One Whose Mind Is Reborn As Truth
# Will Live
# He Will Live Because He Is Truth

---

You can see the world when it is daylight

Likewise, you can see Truth easily

When you have only Truth in your mind

You cannot see Truth

When you have delusions in your mind which is not Truth

Only one whose mind is reborn as Truth

Can see Truth with his mind

Only one who had reached Truth

Can see and know Truth

Because people know only what they have experienced

People who do not have Truth in their minds – they do not

know Truth

Truth is the most supreme

There is no better place beyond Truth

Truth is the place which exists as it is

Only one who becomes this existence

Will live because he is Truth

# Let Only Truth Remain In The Mind

When the mind is clear, there is Truth in the mind

Just as we excrete unnecessary things from our bodies

Let us be rid of the unnecessary false mind from our minds

Though we excrete things from our bodies

Because they are unnecessary

What we need remains in our bodies

Likewise

When we take out the unnecessary falseness from our minds

Only one's true mind will remain

Only he who has a true mind will live

He who has the true mind lives doing true deeds

Because his body and mind are true

# Recovery Of Man's Original Nature

- Man must recover his original nature
- The education which makes humans complete is one that allows people to recover their original nature
- To know your original self
- To know yourself
- It is my fault, my wrongdoing
- To discover the original mind
- To repent
- To return to nature's mind, the original mind
- To become a mind that is as big as the world
- To expand the mind to infinity
- Let us escape from our fixed conceptions and behaviors
- The solution: only one who is reborn as the energy and light of the universe will live

# Only One Who Is Reborn As The Energy And Light Of The Universe Will Live

Existence gives birth to existence

Non-existence cannot create existence

The transformations of existence

Are all creations of the universe

Thus all creations are this existence itself

Every creation is the embodiment of this existence

Which is one

The whole of creation is living

All are alive in the kingdom of this existence

However

Only one who is reborn as the energy and light of the universe

Will live

# Why Don't You Try Cleansing Your Mind?

Do you have a place to go?

Do you have a place to rest?

Do you have a place where you can live forever?

And can you live forever?

If not

Why don't you try cleansing your mind?

# A Rich Mind

If there is yearning in this universe

Then it means that one has yearning in his mind

When the universe becomes his mind

Then the universe becomes oneself, and thus his mind is rich

He will no longer have that yearning mind

His mind would be Truth, which is one

Therefore, both the universe and he will live

# The Years

The elderly live with their oldness

The young live with their youth

All live according to their body's condition

Though people get old their minds do not age

Though their bodies do not do what their minds tell them

Their bodies do not move as their minds will

With the years, many people have come and gone

They have all gone, following their minds

After having lived

According to what they had had in their minds

A person whose mind is reborn as God

Lives forever in the kingdom of God

A person who has the universe in his mind is God

He can live as the energy and light in the kingdom of God

Man can live forever only when

His mind is reborn as the energy and light

He can live forever because only energy and light is Truth

Everything in the universe is light

Which is the spirit of the universe

Everything in the universe is energy

Which is the soul of the universe

And only one who has been born again

As this spirit and soul of the universe

Is that spirit and soul itself

Thus he is one who has completely achieved

The spirit and soul of the universe is God

The person who has God within his mind

Will have no death because he is Truth

Living is for one who is reborn as God

One who becomes God is the living

Everything is God, the Creator

However, humans do not have God in their minds

But have the shadows of memories of their past experiences

And believe these memories are themselves

These are not Truth but mere falseness

But man lives as a slave

According to what that falseness dictates

# People Live According To What They Have In The Mind

This world is also a mind that a person has

A person who has not the true but his false world in his mind

Lives in his false world

People live on their falseness

In the worlds of their own minds

Without the kingdom of Truth in their minds

A person whose mind is Truth

Lives eternally in the kingdom of Truth

Because he has the kingdom of Truth

People live according to what they have in their minds

Likewise, a person who has the true kingdom

Lives in the kingdom of Truth

# Our Bodies And Minds Must Be Reborn As Truth Of The Universe

Even though you come to seek me

If you only look at my shape

You will not be able to find me

When you cleanse your mind, then see your mind

You will be able to find me

Though many come in search of me

Why is it that they leave without being able to?

The reason is because to them, they are better than me

The reason is that their sins and karma are too great

For them to escape from

Therefore they cannot see me

Only when you go into the tiger's den

Can you meet a tiger and catch it

Likewise, only when you come and meet me

Can you find me


The body and the mind are one

And the universe, which is the original mind, and I are one

However, because man's mind sees the universe and humans

As being separate

Man sees shape and the universe separately

When the body and mind of the universe

Comes as a human being

Humans can become that universe, Truth


If you came looking for me, you should meet me

How can you leave without meeting me?

One who meets me has become a true person

He has learned to live forever in the true land

And he lives forever

If you just leave, you will have no place to go

You will die in the false world, following your false mind

Everyone comes to meet me but

They cannot meet me even though I stay as I am

Because they think they are better, more superior than me

And because they have many sins

Yet they do not know this

I even give them the keys and always ask them to come

But they cannot come

Because their sins and karma are too great

A great superior person is one

Who meets me and becomes a new person

A truly great, superior person is one who lives in the new land

The person who lives is the great one

A person who is dead is the foolish one

However people do not know what it means to live or die

People should not make the mistake of not knowing this

They should never ever make that mistake

The universe of this universe tells people

To become the universe, which is Truth, and to live forever

Now is the first and last chance

As a human being who has come to this world

Therefore your body and mind must be reborn

As Truth of the universe now

# Human Completion

Let us return to the mind of the universe

Which is the never-dying God

By discarding our minds

So as to be reborn as the mind and body of the universe

Let us become the universe itself so as to be reborn

That itself is the Creator

That itself is Truth

That itself is the living God

God knows everything in the universe

God is life itself

God is resurrection and eternal life

God is Truth

Human completion means for one to become God

# Drinking

Mountain birds, field birds chirping

In the midst of silence

Only the birds are chirping on the solid frozen river and ground

Sands from the river scatter as strong winds blow

I yearn

But for what I do not know

Maybe it is due to this mood of nature

But there is a yearning that remains in my heart

I drop by the pub

A drunken farmer tilts his glass against his mouth

And repeats the same story over and over again

My cold body melts in the warm cloud of cigarette smoke

My glass is filled with *makkolli* (crude rice wine)

And I have some kimchi on the side

I gulp down the *makkolli* all at once

And breathe a sigh of delight, "Ah!"

I have a bite of kimchi which relieves me

Without a purpose, I sit by the stove

And I warm my hands

With one hand I pour more *makkolli* into my glass

Drink and pour, drink and pour

Eventually the jar of *makkolli* is empty

A bit tipsy, I order another jar

And I begin to get drunk

My frozen heart melts and I become more confident

My tense heart is no more

And my mind opens

I strike up a conversation with the matron behind the bar

Trivial stories about this and that

Complaining about my tough life

All the while my anguish disappears with the *makkolli*

My pain also disappears and I feel good

My confidence appears only when I drink

But as soon as I become sober

That confidence and good feeling has disappeared

I become silent again

My anguish and pain return

Those days of appeasing my regrets with drink

Along with those who had spent their days in the bottle

Have all passed away

And one day I said goodbye to alcohol

The *makkolli* that once melted my body and mind

The *makkolli* that cleared my anguish and pain

I miss that *makkolli* when the wind blows cold

People who I once shared a drink with

Are no longer here

Those moments have become yearnings

I feel empty and age has crept up on me

Without a word, my youth has vanished

As I wandered here and there

There was drink everywhere I went

But I am no longer the free, nameless wanderer

Who could sit and drink at that shabby pub

I have become one who tries to please people

And a person who speaks about Truth

Since there are many who follow me

I am no longer a free man

Yet even among the many, I am a lonely wanderer

I am no longer that person who used to drink

Instead I only speak about Truth

My only wish is to try my best to let people understand Truth

I speak only of Truth because I am Truth itself

Grieving for those who do not have Truth within them

I repeat the same story over and over again

And teach them how to become Truth

The days when I wandered drinking as an ordinary man

Have become a faint memory

Those days are now my nostalgia

Amidst the difficulty of living a lonely life among the crowd

And grieving for man who has not become Truth

I yearn for the freedom of those past days

As the winds blow cold

There is a song that goes, "I am like a bird with no name

I wish I could become a bird and fly away

To that place where no one lives

And live as a bird with no name…"

I used to sing this song in the mountains

It is as if

The person who wrote this song knew how I was feeling

There was one person who heard me singing this song

And must have understood how I felt

Knowing how I wanted to be free because

People could not follow Truth well

I have helped people cleanse the ghosts within them

However, such ghosts betray Truth

Maybe they have yet to be completely cleansed of their ghosts

But among those who practice becoming Truth

I have yet to meet a righteous person

Who is courageous enough to tell me that

They are sorry for having betrayed Truth

It seems that it is not easy for humans

To become the perfect Truth

People are ghosts

Who try to become Truth only for their self-centered selves

Even though I wanted to fly away like a nameless bird

I have continued to protect Truth for over ten years

I will continue teaching Truth until my body passes away

I will continue on until all people live in the kingdom of Truth

I will continue protecting Truth

And live in that kingdom forever

# Our Capacity For Receiving Blessings

Do not blame, cry, and laugh for your blessings

Cry and laugh for me

Then you are the blessed one

If you blame, cry, and laugh for yourself

You are the unblessed

For a person who has falsehood in his mind

His false mind drives out the blessings, and thus

Those blessings cannot remain; blessings do not come to him

One who cries and laughs for me is a person who is blessed

One who laughs and cries for himself

Is the unfortunate one without blessings

Do not try to find blessings outside

When the false mind of the self does not exist

Your true mind is the bowl

Where you can receive your blessings in

When you have a bowl, you can put things in it

Likewise, you can receive blessings

When you have your 'blessings bowl'

A person lives life according to what he has in his mind

Therefore

A person who seeks blessings without having any within

Is a poor fool

The mind is the self, and the body and mind are one

A person speaks and does everything

According to what he has in his mind

Thus, one who does not have Truth in his mind

Cannot gain recognition from others

Because people do not believe him

One who does not have Truth in his mind

Cannot receive blessings even though it is given to him

And does not have a big enough bowl for to receive his blessings

# True Riches

What will you have?

What will you fill your mind with?

People will know the logic that

Everything, including people, lives according to their minds

They will know this

When Truth ripens within them and

When God of wisdom resides within them

No one truly knows

Why man lives and what man needs to have

Alas, what will man have and what will he fill his mind with?

People live in the world

According to what they have in their minds

Therefore because they have falsehood within their minds

They live with burden and pain; they live without rest

Their minds become the falseness itself

And that mind controls them to move and think

That is why people live in burden and pain

And are unable to rest even for a second

The reason and purpose for why humans come to this world

Is to be reborn as Truth and live forever

When they accomplish that purpose

There is freedom and great rest

When you live reborn in the true world while alive

You will know, through wisdom

The reason and purpose for human life

You will know how to live in the world

When you have Truth within

You can live without suffering

Humans worry about

Eating, dressing well, and living in a nice house

But such thing only allow falseness to grow even larger

In one's false mind

True life means to be reborn as the true mind and

To accumulate blessings in the true world

One who is born in the true world works in that world

He will have both the body and mind of God

When he works in that world

When he has blessings in that world

Then those blessings become himself

And he will live by those blessings

What one builds in that world is his

One is rich only when his mind is rich

When one has Truth in his mind, he is truly rich

For one must have riches in order to be rich

When one accumulates his blessings in the true mind

He is not in want of anything

He can live in this land without any insufficiencies

This would be the same even in the world beyond

One lives according to what he has in the mind, and therefore

When one has Truth, which is the true blessing, in his mind

Everything he does is a blessing and all blessings are his

# What Does It Mean To Be Righteous?

That which is alive is living

And everything exists as it is

What sees is the universe and

What hears is also the universe

Every creation is the universe that resembles the universe

And all are living

What a calf cries 'moo'

It is the sound of the universe, a signal from the universe

But no one knows this; no one sees this

The whole of man's mind is the universe

Man's mind is the universe itself

However, people cannot see the universe

Nor do they know that everything and the mind are one

Therefore

They see, hear, do, and speak from their own perspectives

According to what they have in their minds

They see what is going as going, and what is coming as coming

Without knowing that everything just exists as it is

This and that are one

That and this are one

People see everything as being separate

Because they see from their own minds

When they see with the mind of the universe which is one

They will know that everything is one

And that everything is the shape of this oneness

And even that, which has no shape, is of one soul and spirit

And is oneness itself

However, people are deceived by appearances

And thus do not know their origin or their true selves

They do not know what is righteous

To be righteous is to be unbent

To be unbent means to be endless

It means to be living and have no death

It is Truth itself

When you see from the eyes of Truth

You can see everything accurately

You can see as Truth

That which the individual knows and sees has no righteousness

For it is the product of his own subjective delusions

Only Truth is righteous and true

That which Truth sees and knows is righteous because

Truth is that itself and because Truth is unchanging

What is righteous in this universe is only Truth

What is true in this universe is only Truth

Therefore

One who is reborn as the body and mind of this universe

Is a righteous person and everything about him is righteous

However, people cannot see such righteousness

They cannot see it

Because they see from their own point of view

Righteousness is only for one

Who is reborn as the body and mind of the universe

# One Who Is Reborn As The Holy Ghost

Your heavy painful burden

Is due to the things you have stored within your mind

When you cleanse that mind

You will be free from your burdens

You can be completely free from your burdens

When you devote yourself to the Father, to Truth, as Jesus did

Then you are reborn as the Holy Ghost

Which has no painful burdens

Even though you cannot see the burdens of others

All those, who have stored things within their minds

Have burdens

This is sin; this is karma

The state in which there is no world and no self,

Is the state where only Truth, God, exists

One whose mind has been reborn as this existence

Is the one reborn in eternal heaven

When humans are reborn as Truth, God

They will be perfect and complete

Without being reborn as Truth, God

There is no perfect completion

There is no eternal heaven

# Infinity Is...

Infinity is without end

Infinity is the universe before the universe

Infinity is the Creator

Infinity is endlessly large

Infinity is the living existence

Infinity is the existence of Truth

Infinity has no end and no beginning

Infinity is the existence that exists as it is

Infinity is the body and mind of the universe

Infinity is Buddha, God, Haneolim, Allah

Infinity is the origin of all creation; the mother and father of all
creations

Infinity is the original mind of humans

Infinity is the living spirit and body

One who is reborn as this infinite mind will live

As the master of the infinite kingdom forever, without death

Like the nature of infinity, which is to exist on its own

He is the energy and God, itself

Light is life, itself

Light must exist for everything to live

Likewise, when God, which is the light of life, exists

Then everything is Truth

And therefore, everything lives

# Ghosts

"Grandfathers, grandmothers, uncles, and aunts

Lads, lasses

And little children alike

Have you ever seen a ghost?

For I have come to catch ghosts."

Everyone asks me:

"I've never seen a ghost but only heard of it.

Do ghosts really exist?"

Ghost cannot be seen by human eyes

And humans cannot see the ghost

"How can you catch something that cannot be seen?"

Ghosts are

The hundreds of thousands of minds of human beings

Humans live with countless ghosts

But they do not know this because they are ghosts themselves

Ghost uses all sorts of disguises

Therefore it is difficult to tell

Whether it is indeed a ghost or a human being

His face is that of a human being but man is

A ghost that hates

A ghost that likes

A ghost that drinks

A ghost that is crazy

A ghost that loves

A ghost of his enemies

A ghost that pretends to know

A ghost that pretends to be excellent and superior

A pretentious ghost

A ghost that pretends to be soft-spoken and kind

A ghost that thinks it is good-looking

A ghost that thinks it is ugly

A ghost that pretends to be dignified

A ghost that pretends to be intelligent

Using its skill to disguise itself hundred-fold, thousand-fold

The ghost lives only for itself


While ghosts cannot see ghosts

In the eyes of a righteous person, a true person

Ghosts can easily be seen

Also, there are people in the world who are able to catch ghosts

Ghosts do not want to die

And they run away after throwing insults at the true person

Saying that they are the best, that they are right

But in the eyes of a true person

He can see that they act like ghosts

Because they are blinded by their ghosts

He can see right through the ghosts' disguise

I say unto all ghosts: "Do not remain as a ghost. When you become God you can go to the eternal, living heaven."

I say unto all ghosts: "You will know the ways of the world when you become God. If you stay as a ghost, you will die forever. And you will live in hell, in a world that does not exist. Because you do not have the forever-living heaven and wisdom within you, you cannot understand this, nor can you see this. Thus, you live as a ghost, disguising yourself hundred-fold, and thousand fold. Your mind changes day and night."

Eventually the true person who can catch the ghost

Ends up saying the same thing over and over again

To the ghost which changes constantly, day and night

But if the true person

Can manage to keep the ghost from running away

He will one day be able to catch the ghost

The ghost knows that its ghostly life is horrible

The ghost knows that it is not perfect

But still the ghost whimsically goes back and forth

For it is indeed a ghost

This is something that even the ghost catcher cannot help

For which he has no choice but to praise the ghost

And please the ghost

Because he knows that this is the only way

In which the ghost will not run away

Thus, the person who can please the ghost best

Is the one who is the best ghost catcher

I say unto all ghosts: "Let us drive away the ghost and live forever without death, in the world of the divine, with the divine."

I say unto all ghosts: "Do not be stubborn. When you listen to what the divine person says, the ghost can be caught and you can live with the divine."

# How To Speak To People According To Their Situation

An empty chuckle escapes me

I laugh in vain

Ghosts love to be honored and acknowledged

They live only for themselves

Therefore telling the ghost that it is good and that it is right

And being able to speak to people appropriately

According to their situation

While one's true mind remains as it is

It is a tactic, a skillful measure

It is the tactic that a big-minded person uses in order to

Live without conflicts here and there

When the Creator creates everything and lets them live

The Creator lets them live without conflict as one

Yet humans do not know how to live

For they do not have wisdom

Humans do not have the means to do so

Within their own minds

However a big-minded person has the method

The way to get ghosts to listen

Is to praise them for their good qualities

Though they are not actually good qualities

If you dislike them, they will run away

You must praise them

Until they know their own ghostly identities

Until they confess

The world is full of ghosts

Humans, who are all ghosts, seek ghosts outside of themselves

To be friendly with the ghost is the way to catch the ghost

Encouraging them is the way to make them follow Truth

Seeing from the ghost's perspective is the way

To make the ghost not rebel against Truth

# Even Though The Words Are Different, Buddha And God Are The Existence Of Truth And Are One

Both Buddha and God are wisdom. In Buddhism, they say the mind is Buddha, while Christianity says that God exists in the mind. Even though the words are different, Buddha and God are the existence of Truth, and are one.

Truth is the never-changing Creator that existed before the beginning and will go on to exist after infinity. It is the soul and spirit, body and mind, which exists as it is. One whose mind is reborn as this existence can see and know this existence with his mind. Buddha is the true mind; Truth is also the true mind; and God is also the true mind. One who is reborn as the true mind will know this because Buddha, God, is within him.

# Humans Can Become Truth When There Is A Human Who Is Truth

Humans can become Truth

When there is a human who is Truth

The emptiness of Truth gives birth to true existence

The true existence gives birth

To everything as Truth from within the emptiness of Truth

Humans cannot become Truth

If a human who is Truth does not exist

In order for one to become Truth

His body and mind must be born again as Truth

But only Truth knows the method

# Life

Human life passes by like flowing water

Many stories and experiences remain in the heart

Will you go, or will you stay?

Those who go will not achieve

Those who stay will achieve

# Duckweed

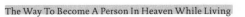

While mountain birds fly

I wander around in the mountains and rivers alone

I sooth my emptiness

By walking around the mountains and rivers

Like duckweed, my mind has no place to firmly plant itself

Nor have I achieved anything in life

Without any achievements and without a place to achieve

I blame the meaninglessness of life

Only I feel trapped in loneliness

And only I have become like floating duckweed of the world

And my mind drifts about, unable to settle

Wood from the mountains contribute the most to the kitchen

There are trees of different ages

And large pine trees here and there

Poor farmers of the country-side

Live in this world

Without complaining, without blaming the world

But I wonder if they know what it is they live for

Indeed, they are diligent and adapt well their environment

They live in complacency

I am the floating duckweed of the world

I want and try to gain something from the world

But there is nothing that fits my mind

Nothing fits my mind for I have countless things in my mind

No matter how much I drink

There is no solution at the bottom of the glass

Without knowing the fundamental ways of how the world is

My mind is like floating duckweed

It may have been that since youth, I did not like the
meaninglessness of life

Among the endless lines of graves in the mountains

Which are the traces of those

Who had once lived and have passed away

I think about the meaninglessness of life

The remains of one who was successful in life is a grave

The remains of one who failed in life is also a grave

They passed away after living lives that were like mere dreams

People who are dedicated to their present lives

Will never understand my mind; they will never know me

I love nature and its silence

So I walk around the mountains and rivers alone

Thinking about my questions and curiosities

About this and that

There were clouds in the clear sky

Winds blowing, rain falling, snow falling

The weather being cold and hot

All are the life of nature

But living was difficult

Because I lived life only for myself

And I knew nothing about life

Though it was only after I became Truth that I realized this

It was no wonder that I did not have the solution before

For the solution was not in my mind

Since I only had falseness in my mind

That is why no matter how hard I looked there was no solution

But now that I have become great nature, the world

My questions about the world have been solved

As I have the origin of the world in my mind

I know the world and I know the will of the world

And my many questions and curiosities are all resolved

# The Difference Between A Ghost And True God

| Ghost | True God |
| --- | --- |
| Has no love, great mercy or compassion | Is love, mercy and great compassion itself |
| Is not the laws of the universe | Is the laws of the universe, itself |
| Is always busy, but has no real results | Only realness remains |
| Ghosts do good deeds because they are told such deeds are good; so those actions are thus false. Ghosts pretend to be good, but his mind is not. | All deeds are pure, true deeds |
| Is not righteous | Is righteous |
| Lives in the world of one's own mind, which he created. Knows, does, and lives according to what he has in his mind. | Is freedom and liberation; is not in want of anything; it has everything in its mind for it is God itself |

| Ghost | True God |
|---|---|
| Is always in wanting, and thus seeks more | Is always content, and therefore just stays |
| Has billions of thoughts that arise | Has no false, delusional thoughts because God knows all |
| Such thoughts are negative | Is positive |
| Is dead | Alive |
| Does not know Truth | Knows Truth |
| Has discernment of what is right and what is wrong | Has no discernment |
| Has billions of minds, such as jealousy, envy, anger, etc | Does not have billions of different minds: no jealousy, envy, anger, etc |
| Is self-centered | Is not self-centered |
| Lives a confined, trapped life | Does not live in confinement |

| Ghost | True God |
|---|---|
| Has no freedom | Is freedom |
| Cannot rest | Always rests |
| Lives in its hell world | Lives in heaven |
| Goes to his false world after its body dies, a false world that does not exist | Exists forever as it is, whether the body is alive or dead |
| Has no wisdom | Has wisdom |
| Has no blessings because the false mind rejects it; blessings cannot enter because of the false mind | Is blessing, itself. Everything goes smoothly and harmoniously |
| A ghost does not know he is a ghost | The true person knows both the ghost and the true person |

# Human Life II

Man, or rather the man's existence, is the mind he has. There is no one in the world whose mind and will are one with that of another because the mind each person has is different. People know, speak, and act according to what they have in their minds. Each person has his own mind world. Therefore, people can live only according to what they have in their minds. No more, no less.

Each person has in his mind what he has experienced since the moment he was born in to the world. That mind becomes his self and he lives in that mind world as the master of his mind world. But that mind is not true, it is false, for which people live mistakenly believing that that which is false is true.

Humans only have falseness; they do not know Truth. Truth knows what is true and what is false, but falseness knows neither. The world one has created is his own false world; and one becomes the master of that falseness, the king of his own false world. Even after he dies, he remains in that false world of his with the mind he has. This is the hell world; this is the false world which is not real. Not only is one king of his own false world; he is the 'devil-king' for he is the greatest demon there is. And when the devil-king's falseness and its false world are destroyed, then the real world appears. The devil-king is self-centered and only knows itself. Therefore the mind that the devil-king has accumulated is its tomb and hell itself.

The reason why man and all creations have come to this world is because Truth created them. Therefore, people and everything are true. However, because of their self-centered minds only humans are dead in this period of growth in the universe. The land of Truth is the world which is beyond the devil-kingdom. The land of God and Buddha exists when the devil-kingdom completely ceases to exist.

The method of Maum Meditation is to completely destroy the devil-king and the devil-kingdom. When you destroy the devil-king's body and mind, and destroy the world of the devil-king, you can be reborn in the kingdom of Truth. This is the method of Maum Meditation.

# The Locations Of
# Maum Meditation Centers

Maum Meditation Centers operate as non-profit
organizations. Currently, there are 203 centers
located around the world.

## THE HEADQUARTERS

Nonsan Main Center

Tel. 82-41-731-1114

407-14, Sangwol-myon, Nonsan-city,
Chungnam, 320-931,
South Korea

## ARGENTINA

Buenos Aires

Tel. 54-11-4633-6598

Av. Carabobo 731 Codigo Postal 1406

Cap. Fed Buenos Aires, Argentina

## AUSTRALIA

Sydney

Tel. 61-2-9763-5340

36 Oxford Rd. Strathfield NSW 2135, Australia

## BRASIL

Sao Paulo

Tel. 55-11-3326-0656

Rua, Afonso Pena, 380, Apt 41 Bom-Retiro,
Sao Paulo, Brasil c.p.f 052458728-03

## CANADA

Toronto

Tel. 1-416-730-1949

33 Everingham Court Toronto Ontario
M2M2J6, Canada

Vancouver

Tel. 1-604-516-0709

7363 Elwell St. Burnaby B.C. V5E 1L1, Canada

## CHILE

Santiago

Tel. 56-2-813-9657

Hanga Roa 739, Recoleta, Santiago, Chile

## ENGLAND

London

Tel. 44-208-412-0134

14 Spinney Close, New Malden, Surrey KT3
5BQ England

## FRANCE

Paris

Tel. 33-1-47-66-29-97

6, rue Saint Saens, 75015 Paris, France

## HONG KONG

Hong Kong

Tel. 852-2572-0107

Flat A-4,10/F, Block A,Elizabeth
House,250-254
Glouceter Road,Causeway Bay, H.K.

## INDONESIA

Jakarta

Tel. 62-21-722-1600

JL.Darmawangsa2, No 25, Kebayoran Baru
Jakarta-Selatan

## ITALY

Genova

Tel. 39-340-496-0027

Piazza Paolo Da Novi 7/4 16129 Genova, Italy

## JAPAN

Fukuoka

Tel. 81-93-601-5102

18-3 Kifunedai Yahata-Nishi-Ku
Kitakyuusyuu-Shi
Fukuoka-Ken, Japan (807-0814)

Osaka

Tel. 81-6-6973-8155

2-19-31 Tamatu Higasinariku Osaka, Japan

Tokyo
Tel. 81-3-6277-9610
Miyuki Bldg. #501, 3-50-15 Sendagi, Bunkyo-
ku, Tokyo, Japan 113-0022

## MALAYSIA
Kuala Lumpur
Tel. 60-3-4257-1482
B-05-05 Ampang Boulavard JLN Airbukit
Taman Ampang Utama
68000 Ampang, Selangor K L, Malaysia

## NEW ZEALAND
Auckland
Tel. 64-9-410-3131
3 Lyttelton Ave. Forresthill, Auckland,
New Zealand

## PARAGUAY
Asuncion
Tel. 595-21-234-237
Tte. Farina e/Pai Perez 1408 Piso 1,
Asuncion, Paraguay

## PHILIPPINES
Manila
Tel. 63-2-832-1402
#4 Lopez Court 2710 Roxas Boulevard
Pasay City Philippines

## SINGAPORE
Singapore
Tel. 65-6222-4171
International Plaza #43-14 10 Anson Road
Singapore 079903

## U.S.A.
Atlanta(Duluth)
Tel. 1-770-232-8630
2565 Davenport Rd, Duluth, GA 30096,
U.S.A.

Atlanta(Sandy Springs)
Tel. 1-678-683-4677
6838 Brandon Mill Rd. Sandy Springs
GA 30328, U.S.A.

Atlanta(Suwanee)
Tel. 1-678-469-1261
3680 George Pierce Ct. Suwanee GA 30024,
U.S.A.

Boston
Tel. 1-617-272-6358
50 Massachusetts Ave. Arlington, MA 02474,
U.S.A.

Chicago(Gold Coast)
Tel. 1-312-526-3437
1023N. Dearborn St. Chicago, IL 60610, U.S.A.

Chicago(Morton Grove)
Tel. 1-847-663-9776
8101 N Central Ave. Morton Grove, IL 60053,
U.S.A.

Dallas
Tel. 1-469-522-1229
3920 Clear Cove Lane, Dallas, TX 75244,
U.S.A.

Denver
Tel. 1-303-481-8844
2542 S Dawson Way Aurora, CO 80014,
U.S.A.

Diamond Bar
Tel. 1-909-861-6888
1311 Longview Dr. Diamond Bar, CA 91765,
U.S.A.

Hawaii
Tel. 1-808-533-2875
1952 Nehoa place Honolulu HI 96822, U.S.A.

Houston
Tel. 1-832-541-3523
1674 Beaconshire Rd., Houston, TX 77077
U.S.A.

Irvine
Tel. 1-949-502-5337
1La flora irvine CA 92614, U.S.A.

Las Vegas
Tel. 1-702-254-5484
7224 Fury Lane Las Vegas NV89128, U.S.A.

Los Angeles
Tel. 1-213-484-9888
226 S. Union Ave. L.A CA 90026, U.S.A.

Maryland
Tel. 1-410-730-6604
4898 Lee Farm ct Ellicott City, MD 21043,
U.S.A.

New Jersey
Tel. 1-201-592-9988
17 Brinkerhoff terr. Palisades Park, NJ 07650,
U.S.A.

New York
Tel. 1-718-353-6678
32-02 150th Place, Flushing, NY 11354, U.S.A.

New York(Long Island)
Tel. 1-516-644-5231
5 York St. Hickville, NY 11801-2319, U.S.A.

New York(Bayside)
Tel. 1-718-225-3472
38-15 216th St. Bayside, NY 11361, U.S.A.

Oakland
Tel. 1-510-922-8550
5601 Carberry Ave. Oakland, CA 94609,
U.S.A.

Orange County
Tel. 1-714-521-0325
7661 West 10th Street Buena Park, CA 90621,
U.S.A.

Philadelphia
Tel. 1-215-635-2371
7449 Overhill Road Elkins Park, PA 19027,
U.S.A.

San Diego
Tel. 1-858-292-6286
8333 Clairemont Mesa Blvd Suite 100
San diego CA 92111, U.S.A.

San Jose
Tel. 1-408-615-0435
3216 Humbolt Ave. Santa Clara, CA 95051,
U.S.A.

Seattle
Tel. 1-253-520-2080
3410 S 272nd St. Kent, WA 98032, U.S.A.

Torrance
Tel. 1-310-534-3598
2210W 230th St. Torrance, CA, 90501, U.S.A.

Valley
Tel. 1-818-831-9888
10434 White Oak Ave. Granada Hills,
CA 91344, U.S.A.

Washington
Tel. 1-703-354-8071
4076 Championship Dr. Annandale,
VA 22003, U.S.A.

http://www.maum.org